"Did I *Really* Say That?"

The Complete Pageant Interview Guide

Written By
Charles J. Margolis

Interview Image Associates, LLC

Cover photography by Sandy Birner
Publisher Interview Image Associates, LLC
For more information, visit www.InterviewImageAssociates.com
or contact cjmargolis@snet.net

For Sharalynn Kuziak, Miss Connecticut 2009

ACKNOWLEDGMENTS

I wish to express my gratitude to Kimberly Fullerton, Pat Greaves and Debbie Midford for their help editing this book. Special thanks to Sally Knowles for the design of the book and Sandy Birner for the cover photography.

Charles J. Margolis earned his master's degree from the University of Hartford. He was a public school art teacher for 35 years. In addition, Mr. Margolis is an accomplished painter, photographer, and poet. Today, he is the executive director of Interview Image Associates, a firm that coaches pageant contestants, politicians, job seekers, and college applicants in all aspects of interview and image enhancement. The author of a poetry book, Class Dismissed: A Teacher Says Goodbye, Mr. Margolis was recently appointed poet laureate of South Windsor, Connecticut, where he currently resides.

For more information, please visit www.InterviewImageAssociates.com.

TABLE OF CONTENTS

TABLE OF CONTENTS

TABLE OF CONTENTS

II. THE ART AND SCIENCE OF INTERVIEW *continued*

TABLE OF CONTENTS

PREFACE

Learn how to tell them a story,
and you'll be a success.

– Don Hewett, news producer,
creator of 60 Minutes (1922–2009)

Several years ago, when I was working as a high school teacher, the closest that I had ever been to a pageant was watching Phyllis George win Miss America 1971 on television. However, on a blustery March morning, a friend called and asked if I could help out by judging a pageant that day, for a member of the judge's panel had just called in sick. For a teacher, Saturdays are more valuable than gold, and giving up an entire day was not what I had planned. Reluctantly, though, I agreed, entering a world in which I would stay involved, to one degree or another, to this day.

I remember being surprised and impressed with the group of young women in this—my first—local pageant. All were attending or had graduated from college, and several had begun promising careers. Yet I was disappointed with the quality of their answers in the interview portion. The majority of responses were predictable, superficial, and impersonal, hardly reflecting their unmistakable intelligence, talent, and grace. Coincidently, I was taking a course in critical thinking at that time, and it occurred to me that I could help these young women improve their thinking and communication skills. I had read several books about communication, attended numerous seminars on the subject, and listened to countless motivational speakers. Actually, the most informative thing I did was to watch great speakers.

After trying to help many contestants with their interviews in various pageants, I had a "Eureka!" moment. I asked myself, what was it that allowed great speakers to communicate so compellingly? I identified that it was their ability to tell a great story—the trick to making audiences be interested in, and often identify with, what they were trying to convey. So, I began instructing pageant interviewees to tell their own stories in their responses. Suddenly, they became fluent, interesting, and expressive—reflecting their true selves.

This was the beginning of my confluent method of pageant

interview. My techniques and approach vary with each contestant, but the idea of getting a woman to tell her own story remains fundamental to my lesson.

As a professional educator and interview coach, I am well versed in pedagogy, the science of teaching. With this knowledge, I was able to develop this original approach to answering interview questions. This book, describing my method, is not a rework of old ideas—the format and content are unique. There are not a lot of footnotes or references. Instead, it is my hope that through this book, contestants will experience new ideas and insights, plus original techniques for interview preparation and presentation.

It is undeniable that the knowledge, self-esteem, and poise gained from learning to interview well will serve contestants long after pageants are well-cherished memories. Whether interviewing for school or a job, giving a speech, or just engaging in conversation, learning how to interview well will be among their most valuable life skills.

For some people, speaking comes as easily as breathing—Winston Churchill; Martin Luther King, Jr.; Barack Obama; Ronald Reagan. Even on the evening news, anchors and reporters deliver information with ease.

Here's their secret: all have worked really hard to become such expert communicators. Public speakers rehearse endlessly, and television personalities are constantly coached and criticized. While talent and charisma are advantages, nothing can replace the hard work that forms the foundation of all quality communication.

All of us would rather work on what we do well and avoid what is difficult. Certainly, interview preparation is more challenging and less fun, than say, choosing an evening gown. However, it has been observed that great athletes spend up to 80% of their practice time practicing the weakest part of their game. As a contestant's competence in interviewing grows, her confidence will be enhanced. In turn, her self-esteem will grow. I always say that self-esteem is like a gymnastics routine. The greater the degree of difficulty, the more points it will be worth.

One of my favorite quotes is from author, inventor, and creativity consultant Roger Van Och: "Everyone has a 'risk muscle.' You keep it in shape by trying new things. If you don't, it atrophies. Make a point of using it at least once a day."

Entering a pageant proves that a contestant is willing to accept a challenge, take a risk, and make positive changes. Interviewing well will further give her the inspiration to fulfill her potential.

It is my firm belief that every pageant contestant can learn how to interview in a way that will earn the respect and admiration of the judges. There is no right way to interview. Just as each person is different, no interview is exactly the same. Think back to my list of great speakers. Each is totally different. There are, however, certain common skills, attitudes, and behaviors that divide mediocrity from excellence.

The key to achieving excellence in an interview is to build on one's personality, strengths, and talents. Whether a contestant is, by nature, gregarious, introspective, intellectual, or intuitive, she inherently possesses qualities that will impress the judges.

I always tell contestants that I gained my greatest insight into interview coaching by reflecting on my own experiences. Every time I made a speech, gave an interview, engaged in a debate, or even taught a class, I thought about what worked and what didn't. Like a surgeon who is performing an operation, I dissected my words, feelings, and thought processes.

A concept that has helped me is the Buddhist practice of mindfulness. This refers to being fully aware of the present moment. Thus, I pay conscious attention to even the most minor details—always. For example, when I watch someone on television, or hear an interview on the radio, I work to understand what is holding my attention. What is attracting or repelling me? It is always more than the words; it is the total picture.

To instruct pageant contestants on how to have a winning interview, I have incorporated this spirit of mindfulness with various strategies and disciplines that I have studied and experienced. For instance, the field of psychology gives insight into how body language, eye contact, and facial expression will subtly influence the judges. Likewise, educational research examines how people learn, and sports provide insights into preparation and motivation. Of course, communication is the foundation upon which the interview is built, creative and critical thinking skills provide the content for answers, and public speaking is rife with techniques for holding the interest of judges. Nutrition directly affects physiology, and even the ancient practice of yoga has yielded methods for calming nerves and focusing attention.

Ultimately, because of this integrated approach, my method is more art than science. It is an amalgamation of knowledge, ability, style, personality, and intangibles. Yet if I had to identify one overall factor that most influences the quality of an interview, it would be attitude. Telltale signs that a contestant is frightened and defensive will be obvious to the judges from the moment that she enters the room. If she is mindful and present and relishes the moment, she will create an interview that both she and the judges will remember.

Thus, this book is also intended to be more than a how-to guide to the pageant interview. It describes a way of living that is confident, bold, and satisfying. This book is designed to demonstrate that the possibilities for personal growth and fulfillment are unlimited. After all, one's attitude determines one's success.

This book contains information, techniques, and strategies for enhancing contestants' personal impact in the interview portion of a pageant. It can be read sequentially or randomly. Each section is actually independent, containing a comprehensive exploration of a single subject. I have tried to write in a way that is easy to understand, succinct, and fun to read. I also love to entertain an audience by sharing personal anecdotes. Wherever applicable, I have included a story that illustrates an idea. However, I have changed all of the names to respect the privacy of the contestants.

In the words of Michel De Montaigne, "I quote others only in order to better express myself." I am an inveterate collector of quotes. They represent the distillation of wisdom from some great thinkers, and I have chosen one quote related to each section to provide inspiration. I suggest that contestants use these quotes as if they were questions; they should discuss each one as though they are talking to the judges. They might even wish to memorize some of their favorite quotes for use during their interviews.

Each section concludes with an interview tip. At first, I called them "interview secrets," but that sounded too dramatic. Each tip provides the kind of advice that only an experienced interview coach can provide, distilling the section into a simple strategy that can elevate interviews. They can be used for quick reference, or like a homework assignment, to study and practice.

It is probably a good idea for contestants to go through the book several times; there is a lot of information to internalize. What seems overwhelming at first will become second nature as they continue to practice what they have learned.

Clearly, this book is primarily intended for pageant contestants. However, judges, business managers, mock interview panelists, and college professors can benefit from it as well. Even job seekers, university interviewees, public speakers, media personalities, and political candidates will (I hope!) find some beneficial lessons.

While we do not always get what we want when we want it, we seem to get what we need. The challenge is to recognize a gift when it is given. I also hope the book helps contestants understand that they can achieve any goal if they are willing to put forth the energy to get it. Most of all, it is my sincerest desire that they learn to accept themselves as the quality people that they are and to honor the beauty in all others. If contestants can carry these lessons with them wherever they go, in whatever they do, their lives will be inspired and fulfilling.

I. WELCOME TO INTERVIEW SCHOOL

1. The Pageantry of the Interview

Learning is wealth that can't be stolen.

– Philippine Proverb

After Linda, a news anchor, won a local pageant, she and I worked on her state pageant interview for 8 months. I had no doubt that she would win the interview award there, and I was thrilled when she lived up to my expectations.

After the pageant, she applied to become a media relations specialist at a well-known financial group. There were more than 300 applicants, and the turn-away rate after the first interview was 90%. After six in-depth interviews, however, she was chosen for the job. She credits the interview skills that she developed for the pageant for helping her land that dream job.

Traditionally, pageant contestants have a reputation for being heavy on good looks and light on intelligence. Some pageants, which feature women who look like Stepford wives, have done little to dispel this perception. Onstage questions that bring generic responses, such as "I wish for world peace" have become standing jokes. Today, however, many pageants attract brilliant competitors who have studied or are studying law, medicine, engineering, art, or international relations. The women whom I have been fortunate to coach have been bright, articulate, and versed on everything from poetry to politics.

The interview is the main event when it comes to pageants. It is an opportunity for the judges to distinguish the person from her fact sheet. In the interview, a contestant has the daunting task of trying to communicate a complex thought in a few short statements. In addition, she has to make her answers interesting and personal. This requires an ability to perceive what is relevant, make connections to personal experiences, and articulate her thoughts. It sounds impossible, but, in reality, we do it all the time. It's called conversation!

Under the scrutiny of the judges, many women become, indeed, like Stepford wives. They abandon their individuality and try to give answers

1

that they think that the judges want to hear. Unquestionably, such responses have contributed to the public perception that pageants are superficial and indulgent.

Putting together a quality interview is like preparing a meal. Combine a base of knowledge with an equal amount of critical thinking, add some communication skills, stir with fluency, and add a liberal dash of personality. Great cooks know that it takes quality ingredients, time, and experience to make a superb meal. With practice and patience, these ingredients will sustain the contestant throughout the pageant interview. Trust me—the outcome will be delicious.

Interview Tip: Use video to evaluate your interview.

2. It's All about You

You are the message.

– Roger Ailes, author, political strategist,
presidential advisor (1940–)

Sheila was very smart, tall, and beautiful. A pre-law student who consistently made the dean's list, she demanded a great deal from herself. We worked on her interview, intermittently, for over 2 years. But each time we practiced, it was like beginning all over again. She would give stereotypical answers that were abstract, impersonal, and just plain dull. Her responses offered little insight into her stellar personality.

During one of our sessions, I said to her, It's all about you! Suddenly, amazingly, it was as though a great weight had been lifted from her shoulders. The strain disappeared from her face, and her interview was energized. Sheila began to enjoy herself! Her answers were infused with personal experience, and were entertaining, animated, and flowed easily.

When a contestant comes to me for coaching, I ask her a few typical interview questions. Initially, most contestants' answers are abstract. They are devoid of personal experience, specific examples, or emotion—totally flat. As a result, contestants begin to sound similar.

The judges want to know the contestant. If they wanted an analysis of world news, they would watch CNN. Of course, to speak intelligently about the world, one must do her homework. However, a factually supported answer will shine with a sprinkling of personalization. For example, when Sheila ran in the state pageant, Senators McCain and Obama were engaged in the Presidential race. The judges asked her to compare the candidates. She did so, displaying her knowledge and analytical ability, but went beyond this by talking about her excitement as a young woman who would be voting in her first election.

Many contestants are advised not to talk about themselves. The fear is that they will sound self-involved or vain. Personalizing answers has the opposite affect. They make the contestant seem accessible and interesting. Think of a piece of mass-produced jewelry compared with something that is handcrafted and one-of-a-kind. Which is more interesting?

3

Nothing will hold the judge's attention like a story that is related to the question. A contestant should seize every opportunity to interject herself into an answer. Even the most mundane question can be a catalyst for a scintillating story by talking about one's experiences and feelings.

Remember, the judges are looking for someone who can relate to people, someone who not only feels good about herself but can also make other people feel good. The contestant who is honest, original, and entertaining will be the woman who wears the crown.

Interview Tip: Try to include something about yourself in every answer.

3. Improving on Nature

To be nobody but yourself in a world that's doing
its best to make you somebody else, is to fight the hardest
battle you are ever going to fight. Never stop fighting.

– e. e. cummings, poet (1894–1962)

I find it mystifying that some pageant directors encourage competitors to take talent lessons, spend months selecting gowns and swimsuits, and go to the gym regularly, but refuse to put the same energy into interview preparation.

I recently had an ongoing debate with a member of a state pageant board of directors on this topic. He argued that interview practice should be avoided, like the flu. He contended that doing any more than a few mock interviews resulted in a contestant appearing coached and unnatural.

To the extent that many contestants do seem rehearsed and give prepackaged answers, he was right. A contestant should be able to think on her feet and respond extemporaneously. However, I believe that becoming a confident speaker requires the same kind of dedication and diligence that elevates performance in any discipline.

Athletes are coached; they perform drills and practice until their skills and strategies are second nature. Still, they have to adapt to unexpected circumstances in every game. It is precisely because repetition has honed their skills to razor-sharpness that they can respond to every contingency. In my experience, appearing comfortable, confident, and natural in an interview is usually the result of training and a lot of practice. Good interview training teaches the contestant how articulate her thoughts, views, and feelings. It incorporates critical thinking skills and different ways of responding to questions. Practice techniques, such as mock interviews, help the contestant gain confidence and experience. Thorough preparation makes a pageant interview feel as natural as a conversation between friends.

When I judged pageants, I liked to ask unusual questions. That way, I was able to access the contestant's ability to respond spontaneously.

Although it is true that many pageant questions are used frequently, no one can or should try to predict every question. The contestant who depends on rehearsed answers will appear rigid and programmed. Also, when confronted with the inevitable unexpected question, she may not know what to say and panic. The result can be a disaster. Through training and a lot of practice, a contestant can enter an interview feeling like she can answer any question.

Interview Tip: Athletes, who replicate high-intensity race conditions during practices, improve their actual race times by 10%. So, practice the interview as though it was the actual pageant.

4. It Takes More than Talent

Use what talents you possess; the woods would be very silent if no birds sang there except those that sang best.

– Henry Van Dyke, author, poet, essayist (1852–1933)

Diana radiated energy, like a small sun. Her dynamic personality and experience as a communications major made it likely that she would win the interview award. Yet on stage, it was obvious that she had spent a lot more time at the gym than at the podium. Although she did have a natural gift for speaking, that wasn't enough.

Most contestants practice what they are good at doing and neglect what is difficult. Even talent has its limits. There needs to be a balance between reinforcing what a contestant does well and improving the areas that need extra work.

Once, after the first meeting of all contestants, I remember that one woman complained that everyone else had "so much talent." It is true that the pageant interview comes easily to some. However, a recent analysis of high performers in a range of activities—piano, chess, hockey, soccer, computer science, etc.—revealed that talent is less important than training and practice. Although talent can put a person on the fast track, making it possible to reach high levels of performance sooner, other factors have equal or greater influence over what one is able to achieve.

None of us are duplicates of one another, not even identical twins. The interview is about expressing individuality. Thus, whether a contestant finds the interview easy or challenging, how she prepares for it—not innate talent—will make the difference between success and mediocrity.

Interview Tip: According to research, talent accounts for 25% of a person's success in any given endeavor. Focus on the 75% you can control.

7

5. Preparation, Practice, Persistence

Failing to plan is planning to fail.

– Proverb

When LPGA champion Annika Sörenstam hits a golf ball, she does not consciously think about keeping her head down, straightening her left arm, and following through. Instead, years of practice have given her "muscle memory." While the analogy is not quite the same for the pageant interview—because a contestant must always think before she answers—preparation does allow a contestant to respond well spontaneously, just as she would during a regular conversation.

Sarah had the talent, figure, and determination to win the state pageant. What she didn't have was the interview skills. Her abysmal interview cost her that title the previous year. We began working together shortly after that pageant. Sarah and I talked about everything under the sun and did one-on-one mock interviews until she was ready to fall over. These were stressful interviews that challenged both her ability to answer and her poise under fire.

Sarah won every category in the state pageant, including interview, that year.

University of Connecticut woman's basketball coach Geno Auriemma says that games are "won and lost in practice." Interview preparation is a marathon, not a sprint. Go at your own pace, but don't ever stop. One would not expect to play the piano well without practicing regularly. Be persistent, and you will reach your goal.

Interview Tip: There is a direct relationship between interview preparation and success.

6. My Fair Lady: Developing New Mindsets

There is no elevator to success. You have to take the stairs.

– Anonymous

When I began teaching, Pygmalion in the Classroom, by Robert Rosenthal and Lenore Jacobson, became popular among educators. The title comes from George Bernard Shaw's play, Pygmalion, which was adapted into the Broadway musical My Fair Lady. The book cites a research experiment in which teachers were told that one group of elementary students was brighter than another—but the truth was that this assertion was false. However, the students, who were identified as being smarter, did perform better, but not due to innate intelligence. The teachers unconsciously behaved in ways that contributed to the success of the "brighter" group; the teachers were responsible for giving the students a covert message about what they were capable of doing. What the students came to believe about themselves is known as a "self-fulfilling prophecy."

The lesson in this is that a contestant must have high expectations for herself. I am not talking about overconfidence or blatant arrogance. If she has prepared properly, she has every reason to anticipate a good interview. Further, if she believes that the judges want her to do well, she will have an interview that is consistent with her beliefs. However, if the contestant approaches the interview believing that everything will go wrong, it will. If she thinks that the judges will be hostile, she will create a negative self-fulfilling prophecy.

Changing a mindset is a daunting task. The brain tends to organize experience and information into neat packages, marked DO NOT DISTURB. Mindsets result from early childhood development, beliefs, and experiences. They have a direct relationship to self-esteem. The best way a contestant can develop a positive mindset about herself and her expectations for the pageant interview is to understand what she needs to do to be successful. She must create a self-fulfilling prophecy that holds her accountable for the highest standard of interview performance. Like Eliza Doolittle in My Fair Lady, she can transform her

11

interview into an elegant, convincing presentation with the right training, effort, and mindset.

Interview Tip: You need to believe you can win in order to win.

7. Inner Voice

If you could only sense how important you are to the lives of those you meet; how important you can be to the people you may never even dream of. There is something of yourself that you leave at every meeting with another person.

– Fred Rogers, educator, minister, television host (1928–2003)

I used to tell my students that people react to challenges in one of two ways. Given a problem or goal, most people immediately offer every possible reason why they cannot possibly reach the goal. Presented with the exact same situation, there is a small minority of people ask, "What do I need to get there?"

I often refer to a contestant's wanting to be there. This is a mindset—a group of beliefs, values, or accepted behaviors held by an individual or group. I know a woman who wanted a job as a teacher. She interviewed in one district. When she was not hired in that district, she adopted the mindset that she couldn't get a job in any district. Can you imagine an author who sends a manuscript to only one publisher, then quits writing because of a rejection? Chicken Soup for the Soul, by Jack Canfield and Mark Victor Hansen, was rejected 140 times before finding a publisher. To date, it has sold 112 million copies. I think we can safely say there are 140 publishers mumbling, "What was I thinking?"

It is estimated that a person has 150,000 thoughts every day. Unfortunately, many of these are negative. Additionally, we tend to ruminate on these negative thoughts, which make them seem larger than they are. In contrast, positive self-talk can help a pageant interview. A contestant needs to program her mind to believe in a good outcome. Her inner voice is like a road. By following it, she will reach her destination.

Interview Tip: Just before you fall asleep, review what you have accomplished that day.

DID I REALLY SAY THAT?

8. Mindfulness: Being Present

Mindfulness is the aware, balanced acceptance of the present experience. It isn't more complicated than that. It is opening to or receiving the present moment, pleasant or unpleasant, just as it is, without either clinging to it or rejecting it.

– Sylvia Boorstein, Psychotherapist,
yoga teacher, health practitioner (1936–)

I used to teach a course called "Exploring Your Creativity." It was about the creative process as expressed in every human endeavor. One of the characteristics of creative people is their ability to notice the common things most of us usually take for granted.

When something that has gone unnoticed enters consciousness, a person becomes mindful. Try this simple exercise: brush your teeth with the opposite hand or wear your ring on another finger for a day. Being aware of what is going on, both inside oneself and externally, opens perception and promotes creativity.

The concept of mindfulness can be found in Buddhist, Native American, yoga, and Taoist practices. Its essence involves living in the present moment—an intentional, active attention to now. Ordinarily, our minds jump all over the place. We are constantly bombarded by distractions, memories of the past, and anticipation of the future. Noise like this interferes with our awareness of the present. Mindfulness quiets inner chatter and focuses our attention. It can mitigate stress, lower blood pressure, and boost immune function. Being mindful allows awareness of what one is doing and the potential to change it, if that is what she chooses to do.

What does mindfulness have to do with the pageant interview? As many have said in many different ways, the past is done and the future is uncertain; we have only the present. Yet for many pageant contestants, the interview is about what has happened or what might happen. Worrying about whether they have sufficiently prepared is to think about the past. Fearing what can go wrong is to anticipate the future. Negative thinking seems to come easily and is why contestants often become nervous.

Mindfulness requires that a contestant becomes an observer who sees only the present. Quieting the internal chatter lets her listen to the judges' questions and connect with the flow of the interview. Being mindful requires purpose and practice.

Interview Tip: Learn to want to be where you are.

9. Becoming Mindful

Normally, we do not so much look at things
as overlook them.

– Alan Watts, philosopher,
teacher, writer (1915–1973)

Golfers remind me of Don Quixote, always in pursuit of the mythical perfect round. Everything can be going well, but one badly hooked ball or a single missed putt can change everything. Doubt can easily replace confidence, and internal chatter can disrupt concentration. The rare golfer is the one who can take one shot at a time, without dwelling on what has happened or worrying about what will come.

Like a golfer, the interview contestant will inevitably say something that she would say differently if she could do it over—known as a "mulligan" in golf. However, a contestant must learn to put aside the previous answer and be present for each question. She must, essentially, learn to be mindful. Focus externally. One of the greatest impediments to mindfulness is overthinking, as it makes one self-conscious and anxious. To be mindful is to be in the here and now. A contestant should focus on what is going on in the interview, not in her head. If she is mindful, she can erase overthinking and thus, her self-consciousness. Her true personality can then shine through.

Savor the moment. A good piece of dark chocolate is better if one lets it melt in the mouth, instead of chewing it as fast as possible. Similarly, mindfulness allows a contestant to savor experiences and enjoy them as they happen. And, if a contestant remains in the present moment, her fears will melt away faster than that piece of chocolate.

Accept the present. Some things, like interview preparation, can be controlled. Other things, such as the questions asked by the judges, cannot. Being mindful allows a contestant to let go of her fears and expectations by focusing on what is occurring in the moment.

Notice new things. Most of the time we are like cars on cruise control, so lost in our thoughts that the present moment passes unnoticed.

This is called habituation. As a contestant enters an interview, filled with instructions on how to walk, talk, and speak, the immediacy of the moment goes unnoticed. To be mindful, notice new things. What are the judges wearing? How is the room configured?

Interview Tip: Treat each moment as if it will never come again.

10. The Zen of Interview

Your mind will answer most questions if you learn to relax and wait for the answer.

– William S. Burroughs, novelist,
essayist, poet (1914–1997)

I was sent to evaluate a 3-day wilderness adventure trip with a group of other teachers and social service personnel. After a freezing night in a paper-thin sleeping bag, I awoke too early with the sun. A morning jog ended suddenly when I stepped in hole, soaking my new running shoes with mud. After a day of hiking in the heat, I spent the evening recovering from hypothermia.

The next 2 days were a series of demanding physical and mental challenges. As we walked through the forest, my new hiking boots began rubbing the back of my ankles raw. Seeing my obvious distress, one of our leaders, named Ashanti, joined me. To this day, I remember his simple advice, "Milk the moment."

Over time, I came to understand his meaning. Every experience presents the opportunity to learn something new. Paying attention to what I was feeling—and how I responded in the present moment—did teach me a new thing about myself. Thanks to my wilderness adventure trip, I can now proudly say that I have the ability to withstand a whole lot of physical and mental challenges!

Being present will heighten awareness, and the internal chatter that comes from anticipation will be silenced. Much like meditation, the mind will become an empty receptacle ready to be filled. This may sound counterintuitive, since most contestants are counseled to have a zillion answers ready to recall. To achieve this, a contestant has to trust herself, give up trying to control everything, and allow the interview to unfold. In less esoteric terms, it means wanting to be exactly where one is.

I call this the "Zen of Interview," a mind state that allows answers to flow as freely as casual conversation. If a contestant is experiencing this state, she will

- experience a sense of well being,
- be excited rather than nervous,
- be anxious to share her story with the judges,
- feel excited about having six people who focus only on her,
- lose her sense of time,
- know that she has something important to say, and
- enjoy the experience.

Interview Tip: Trust yourself enough to give up control.

11. Swimming with the Tide

People who learn to control inner experience will be able to determine the quality of their lives, which is as close as any of us can come to being happy.

– Mihaly Csikszentmihalyi, Author,
Psychologist (1934–)

One rainy morning in November, I ran in a 5K race. About 1 mile into the race, I caught up with a guy who looked like he might be in my age division. Knowing that winning a medal might depend on me finishing ahead of him, I matched his pace. For the next 2 miles, we ran stride for stride. I was running as fast as I could, unable to speak, spit, or do anything but survive. Strangely, I felt great. My breathing was deep and regular; my stride was full and strong. Though I was performing at peak efficiency, I felt a heightened awareness. I was even able to look around and enjoy the scenery. It was as if I was riding on my legs.

I was in the flow.

The term "flow" was first defined and extensively researched by psychologist Mihaly Csikszentmihalyi. In sports, it is often referred to as the "zone." I am a huge fan of the UConn women's basketball team. It is amazing how, when a basketball player is in the zone, every shot seems to go in.

To reach the zone, the task has to match the upper limit of one's ability level. For instance, I never could have run with the winner of the race; that was beyond my ability. Trying to do so would result in a lot of pain and ultimate failure. Instead, I had a clear, achievable goal: to win a medal in my age division. Second, achieving flow requires the potential for immediate feedback so behavior can be adjusted accordingly. In my example, running next to my competition gave me instantaneous information. I could hear his labored breathing and knew he was working as hard as me.

Being in the flow is the best possible condition for the pageant interview. Experiencing it, contestants have told me that they felt like their interview was fun and easy. Invariably, they comment on how the interview seemed to be so short.

Being in the flow is also characterized by a sense of satisfaction. When a contestant I have coached is being interviewed, I nervously await her phone call. As soon as I hear her voice, I know if she has been in the zone.

Interview Tip: Trying too hard can actually sabotage your efforts. Once you have begun the interview, just let it happen.

12. Apples and Oranges Can Make You Nuts

Why compare yourself with others? No one in the entire world can do a better job of being you than you.

– Susan Carlson, minister, nurse, health practitioner

By the second day of the state pageant, something had changed for Laura, an intelligent and attractive opera singer. She had become totally despondent, often sitting in the back of the auditorium and crying. No amount of reassurance or cajoling could lift her misery. She had lost her confidence and, with it, her composure. It began when she concluded that a few dancers had greater stage presence, and it snowballed on from there. Comparing herself to her competitors was a huge mistake.

From that point onward, her loss of assuredness affected everything that she did. After the pageant, I spoke to one of the judges. She told me that Laura appeared stiff and uncomfortable onstage. Her lack of poise was evident.

Given that we can, at best, only make an educated guess at what the judges will like, many contestants inevitably begin comparing themselves with their competition. While this is quite natural, it is like comparing apples and oranges. Sure, anyone can identify a particularly talented singer or graceful dancer. But, don't count out that baton twirler—she may win the title.

While there are standards for performance—especially in the area of talent—what will ultimately impress the judges is elusive. More than once, I have been completely surprised by the judges' selection. Events such as swimsuit and evening gown are subject to personal taste. Furthermore, we simply don't know how each contestant has performed in the private interview.

Instead of comparing herself to others in the competition, a contestant should concentrate on trying to be the best that she can be. Making comparisons with other contestants will only have a detrimental effect on her psyche.

Interview Tip: Have you ever seen an apple try to become an orange?

13. Charisma: The Chemistry of Personal Magnetism

How can you have charisma? Be more concerned about
making others feel good about themselves than you are
making them feel good about you.

*– David P. Reiland, business executive
(1954–)*

Every November, as the anniversary of the assassination of President John F. Kennedy approaches, I remember how President Kennedy once infused the country with a sense of hope and youthful energy. He was handsome and spoke with an engaging Boston accent that was widely and affectionately imitated. In short, President Kennedy had charisma.

Charisma is that magical quality that makes some people instantly likeable. These are the kind of people with whom everyone wants to talk at a party, leaders who command respect, and congenial people who make everyone feel comfortable. Is their magnetism a gift of birth or a learned behavior? According to some scientists, charisma is 50% genetics and 50% training. My experience as a pageant interview coach has demonstrated that charisma results from a series of behaviors that almost anyone can learn.

Charisma can elevate the level of a pageant interview. Note that I am not talking about the quality of answers; I am referring to the overall impression that a contestant gives to the judges.

Charisma is like a soup. Many individual ingredients go into the mix, but it is the combination that yields the full flavor. Charisma is an amalgamation of open body language, speaking pace, ideas, eye contact, feedback, and the ability to listen, all of which I will talk about in greater depth later in the book. Charismatic individuals also share a sense of empowerment. That is, they convey the feeling that they are confident, in charge, and have a vision of where they are going. Charismatic individuals are magnets that attract people to them.

Contestants can raise the level of their interview by incorporating some of the following behaviors and attitudes.

25

- **Openness.** Stand up straight, make eye contact, and smile.
- **Energy.** Pronounce each word clearly, and vary the tone and tempo of speech.
- **Competence.** Articulate ideas clearly.
- **Individuality.** Be positive, upbeat, and friendly.
- **Confidence.** Deliver answers that are consistent with one's beliefs and values.

Interview Tip: In no small measure, charisma is the result of being self-assured and having a strong sense of self.

14. Charm School

A beauty is a woman you notice; a charmer
is one who notices you.

– Adlai Stevenson, governor, presidential
candidate, ambassador (1900–1965)

Isis was smart, serious, and focused. After a year of hard work, her interview was quite good. Still, it lacked something. She was too serious, too stoic, and too impersonal. For a couple of weeks, I searched for the right word to define the quality that I wanted her express. Then, it came to me. When you go into the interview, I told her, I want you to charm the judges.

She did. Charm and charisma are not the same. Charm is outwardly oriented, while charisma is more of an intrinsic quality. Charm brings pleasure to other people, while charisma is a kind of personal attraction. Charm is related to how one makes people feel; charisma is about how people feel about someone else.

True charm is not false or a set of old-fashioned rules. It comes from having genuine concern for the comfort and welfare of other people. This is why people respond emotionally to charming people. There is an instantaneous feeling of rapport. Often, the comment heard about such a person is that she feels like a close friend.

The charming contestant will make the judges' job easier. She will make them feel at ease. Nothing is quite as charming as someone who can laugh at her own foibles. Charming people share themselves through personal stories, are upbeat, and go out of their way to be considerate. I guess that the secrets of charming individuals are really not secrets, after all:

- display good manners,
- share personal anecdotes,
- show warmth and humor,
- acknowledge good question or observations by a judges, and
- smile and laugh often.

Interview Tip: Charm the judges with humility, humor, and honesty.

15. The X Factor

In the future, everyone will be famous for 15 minutes.

– Andy Warhol, artist (1928–1987)

Brianna asked me what the pageant directors mean when they say that they want an "It Girl." I explained that an It Girl is the contestant who possesses that something extra—the "X factor." Similarly, when I was in college, my mentor told me, "I can't tell you what good art is, but when I see it, I know it." There are many ways of knowing, most of which occur beneath the conscious level. The X factor, which separates one contestant from the others, involves more than talent or good looks. It is a mix of personality, behavior, and ability-related characteristics. Some of these can be learned.

The X factor is unusual because one person rarely exhibits the whole package. For a pageant contestant, the X factor can include charisma, physical attractiveness, a dynamic personality, talent, intrinsic motivation, and stage presence. The ability to influence others—known as "social potency"—is an additional factor. Another inherent quality associated with the X factor is "expressive control"—the ability to impress and entertain others. Being extroverted and having behaviors that are so well matched that they create an exceptional impression are a rare combination.

The X factor involves a critical balance between displaying unique abilities yet still being able to make a connection with ordinary people. People identify with a contestant who tries hard. It affirms the sense that she deserves her talents. Another important, but often overlooked, feature of the X factor is humility. A sense of gratitude makes a contestant sympathetic, genuine, and likable. Conversely, too much self-confidence appears arrogant. The X factor is a delicate balance of opposing characteristics.

The X factor involves personality traits that can be cultivated by adapting certain attitudes and behaviors. While the X factor is elusive, when it's there, everyone is aware of it.

- Learn to accept criticism.
- Appreciate oneself.
- Capitalize on personal strengths.
- Be agreeable.
- Develop social skills.
- Take risks.
- Show humility.

Interview Tip: Believing in yourself leads others to believe in you.

16. Act I: When Role-Playing Isn't a Game

To be a great champion you must believe you are the best. If you're not, pretend you are.

– Muhammad Ali, world heavyweight boxing champion (1942–)

Yvonne was one of the most competent and engaging women whom I have ever known. A clinical social worker, drug and alcohol abuse counselor, and expert in group interaction, she could negotiate Manhattan's business and social networks with equal facility. She became a leader in women's business development and a contributor to the online edition of Cosmopolitan. Yvonne seemed at home in every situation.

So, I was astounded when she told me that there was a time in her life when the mere thought of dealing with a group of people—even at a party—would make her feel like "hiding in the closet." To get over this, she began observing people who seemed comfortable in social situations. She identified the behaviors that attracted people to them. Then, she practiced by role-playing. When she went to a party, she would employ these behaviors and pretend that people liked and were drawn to her. Guess what? They were. Soon enough, the practice became a way of life.

When a contestant is being interviewed, she may feel stressed, anxious, or insecure. One way to overcome these feelings is to role-play—to pretend. Just as actors identify with the role that they are playing, a contestant who is not particularly outgoing can assume the persona of someone who is extroverted during an interview. When the "play" is over, she then returns to her normal identity.

Gillian and I worked on her interview for several years. She would improve, backslide a little, and then improve even more. Each time she was better, until one night she was as good as I have ever seen. Out of curiosity, I asked her what was different. She told me that she stopped thinking and worrying about her answers. I asked her whether this behavior was natural or acting. "Both!" she replied. In her interview role, Gillian was confident and fluent.

31

If a contestant is stressed by the thought of an interview, she should role-play exactly how she wants to appear before the judges. When a practice interview is going well, she should make a conscious effort to remember how it felt. During the next interview, try to retrieve those feelings. Remember, the advantage of role-playing is that the contestant controls the character.

Interview Tip: Role-playing is not an act.

17. Heroes and Role Models—Choose Carefully

Without heroes, we are all plain people and
don't know how far we can go.

– Bernard Malamud, author
(1914–1986)

As a teacher, I always cautioned my students to choose their heroes carefully. I was lucky to grow up in a home where my brother was my hero. Unfortunately, for a lot of people, their heroes have feet of clay. Athletes who use performance-enhancing drugs and celebrities with disastrous personal lives have become all too common as heroes. Talent is absolutely no indication of a person's character.

"Who is your role model?" is one of the most frequently asked questions in a pageant interview. It is a good question but usually brings a predictable response. The majority of contestants answer "my mom" or "Jesus." There is nothing wrong with these responses, but there is some question of originality. Now, if her mother or anyone else is a contestant's role model, certainly she can talk about that person. However, it is always a good idea that a contestant separates herself from the other contestants by giving a unique response.

I was once asked to be on an interview panel for a group of Junior Miss pageant contestants. We presented the same role model question to each of the girls. One contestant stood up, paused for a moment, and then gave one of the most memorable answers that I have ever heard. She did, indeed, identify her mother as her role model—but the caveat was that her mother was her reverse role model. Her mother conceived her at a young age and had not always set the best example. Learning from her mother's mistakes, this young woman demonstrated extraordinary acceptance, insight, and maturity.

In psychology, there is a concept known as "modeling." It refers to a person demonstrating the correct way to behave or to perform a particular task. As such, a child's first role model is usually the parent. As children become older, their spheres of influence widen. When I was 14, I wanted to be like Jimmy Brown, the great Cleveland Browns running back. Now, I particularly admire Oprah Winfrey and Bill Cosby because they seem to care about other people. Plus, each has handled the pressures of fame and wealth without losing their core values.

Remember, a contestant's choice of heroes and role models says a lot about who she is and what she aspires to become. Heroes and role models do not have to be famous or celebrated. One of my heroes is a friend whom I have known since the first day of high school. Ordinary people, who face the challenges of life with courage and purpose, are real heroes. They are all around us.

Interview Tip: Look for role models in unexpected places.

18. Searching for Jerry Seinfeld

Laughter is the shortest distance between two people.

– Victor Borge, comedian, pianist,
conductor (1909–2000)

I am a habitual viewer of C-SPAN2 Book TV. I know how nerdy that sounds, but it is so. I love hearing authors talk about their books, research, and creative process. I also like to watch how well the authors speak before an audience. For the most part, they are better writers than speakers. One Sunday, Janine Turner was the guest author. She is an actress who formerly starred on Northern Exposure. Every so often, during her talk about her book, Ms. Turner would burst into ebullient laughter. It was as though she just couldn't contain her enthusiasm and pure joy. She was memorable and a delight to watch.

In 1965, Dr. Bernie Segal began using laughter as a therapy for treating his cancer. Subsequently, he became a champion for using humor therapeutically in the treatment of many diseases. Patients watched funny movies and listened to jokes. Now it is well known that laughter releases endorphins that mitigate pain and serotonin, which makes us feel good.

On average, people laugh 17 times per day. People who laugh readily are more socially active and affable. Laughter involves both the right and left hemispheres of the brain. The left side recognizes the words, while the right side responds to the incongruity or relationship that makes something funny. Humans of every age and culture love to laugh.

Eliza had an irresistible laugh. She laughed easily and often. Her laughter was neither self-conscious nor contrived. I had no doubt that Eliza would win interview, due, in no small measure, to her infectious laugh. Plus, it made being in her company always a pleasant experience. During her interview, I was told that the judges' laughter could be heard coming from the interview room. Yes, she did win that interview award.

In a pageant interview, laughter gives a huge amount of nonverbal information to the judges. It puts them at ease. I'm not talking about performing a comedy routine or telling jokes. Nor am I referring to the self-conscious giggle that punctuates the end of some people's sentences. A little self-enfacing humor—the kind that pokes gentle fun at one's foibles—shows the judges that a contestant has a sense of humor.

Genuine laughter can do more for an interview than any other single thing. A contestant should laugh whenever and as often as she can.

Interview Tip: Laughing at yourself doesn't make you a fool.

19. The Perfect Exercise

> Every time you smile at someone, it is an action of love,
> a gift to that person, a beautiful thing.
>
> – *Mother Teresa of Calcutta (Agnes Gonxha Bojaxhiu), catholic missionary, nobel prize winner (1910–1997)*

I was waiting to be interviewed about my poetry on a television program. For an instant, I wondered if I could talk about my book for a whole hour. Quickly, I put the thought aside and smiled.

I was pondering a relatively new piece of clinical research that had grabbed my attention. It had been assumed that facial expression was a direct result of feeling emotion—that is, to smile, one had to feel good. Research found, however, that facial expression doesn't just express emotion—it can also shape it. Although it seems counterintuitive, the physical act of smiling can change the way a person feels. When a person holds a smile for a short while, the feeling of happiness becomes greater. It is believed that physiological changes in the face induce biochemical changes associated with the emotion.

Imagine having the ability to change your mood and the mood of others in an instant. It would be like having some sort of superpower! Well, this is not science fiction—it is actual science.

So, as I waited for the taping to begin, I made a conscious effort to smile. Throughout the interview, I maintained my happy expression; sure enough, the interview went smoothly. Many of the people who watched the program told me, "You looked like you were really comfortable."

Ending interview answers with a smile makes the interviewee feel that he or she has been successful. After all, smiling is contagious. Smile at people, and they are likely to smile back. A smile is a universal language. It makes a person appear more attractive, invites interaction, boosts the immune system, and relieves stress.

If a contestant wants to feel good and perform well during her pageant interview, she should let her smile speak.

Interview Tip: Your expression is like a map of your emotional landscape.

20. Passion: The Fuel that Powers Interviews

Passion is energy. Feel the power that comes from
focusing on what excites you.

*– Oprah Winfrey, TV personality, actress,
producer, philanthropist (1954–)*

Bob was a guest on our cable talk show, Video Journal. After graduating from an Ivy League school with a degree in physics, he began a career in research. Finding that unfulfilling, he became a social worker. For fun, Bob began working at a local cable television station. This was in the early days of cable access TV. He learned how to use a camera, as well as editing and production methods. More importantly, Bob found his calling. He began making movies. His choice of subjects—alcoholism and sexual abuse—reflected his abiding concern for social welfare. In time, Bob won prestigious awards for his films. His message has resonated with me since that interview: "Find your passion." Do what you love, and you will always be a success.

To have passion, you must love. Enthusiasm is inexorably tied to passion. Max, another guest on the show, was a movie and TV actor. In fact, he appeared in the Leave It to Beaver pilot and starred with Marilyn Monroe in Niagara. From my first question to the moment that the 30-minute program ended, Max talked without interruption. He was so enthusiastic that he carried the entire program with his memories and stories. His zest for life came through in his energetic discussion.

A contestant's passion and enthusiasm are the fuel that powers the pageant interview. The judges are looking for someone who is excited about being a queen. Someone who has passion for her platform will inspire others to follow her.

Passion is a creative force that comes from the inside and is manifested on the outside. To exhibit such passion, a contestant must focus on the following.

- Energy level. Use movement and expression.
- Voice inflection. Vary the intensity, intonation and tone.

- Facial expression. Add emphasis and energy with animated features.
- Hand gestures. Allow her hands to speak freely.
- Posture. Make herself tall.
- Eye contact. Remember that eye movement is energy.

Interview Tip: Don't be afraid to show your enthusiasm.

21. High Voltage: Interview Energy

The higher your energy level, the more efficient
your body. The more efficient your body, the better you
feel and the more you will use your talent to produce
outstanding results.

– Tony Robbins, self-help author and
success coach (1960–)

The motivational speaker mesmerized his audience. "Step up!"
he commanded the thousands of business executives who had paid
considerable sums to hear him speak. In one voice, they echoed his
mantra, over and over. Dynamic speakers like him can ignite a crowd.
Energy is contagious. It makes people likable, and likeability is an integral
part of the pageant interview.

The Law of Conservation of Energy says that energy can neither
be created nor destroyed—it can only be transformed from one state to
another. Physical and psychological energy are interrelated. If a contestant
is tired or upset, those emotions will drain her physical energy. However,
being passionate and excited can create physical vitality. Certainly, there is
a body–mind connection.

People are like rechargeable batteries. They are capable of
gathering energy from many sources. Exercise, for example, releases
chemicals, like serotonin, that make people feel good. Thoughts, too,
have the capacity to raise or to lower energy. Negative people and
situations are energy vampires, which drain life force.

For a contestant, feelings are the guide to identifying positive
sources of energy. Dwelling on what can go wrong creates fear and saps
vitality. Recalling events that engender feelings of competence and
confidence energize. People who like what they are doing have energy.

Each person has an optimal level of energy. Some contestants
are more effervescent than others, but every contestant must find a level
of energy that is congruent with her personality. If she is too laid back, then
she needs to turn up the voltage. For the contestant who comes on too

strong, dial it back a bit. There is a stereotype of the over-the-top pageant contestant, who supercharges the interview with kinetic energy. While a hyperactive interview can be exciting, it is only one of many interview styles.

The interview contestant is a performer. The judges are her audience. She can convey a sense of vitality through her voice, gestures, and facial expressions. She must use to learn to use her voice as a tool of expression. Change the volume, tone, and inflection. Large movements of the hands and arms are a manifestation of energy. The face is a mirror of intrinsic energy.

I have calculated the equation for interview energy: Purpose + Passion x Enthusiasm = Interview Energy.

Interview Tip: Try rating the interpersonal energy of news anchors and game show hosts on a 1–10 scale. Listening to radio DJs will also provide insight into how the voice—without visual clues—can convey energy. Learn to recognize how energy levels influence perception.

22. Motivation: Joys of the Journey and Rewards of the Destination

Do you do it for money, honey? The answer is no. Don't now and never did. Yes, I've made a great deal of dough from my fiction, but I never set a single word down on paper with the thought of being paid for it…I have written because it fulfilled me…I did it for the pure joy of the thing. And if you can do it for joy, you can do it forever.

– Stephen King, author (1947–)

Ron and I have been friends since high school. One summer, when he was home from college, I taught him to play chess. He still remembers the shocked look on my face the first time that he won. By the end of season, he was winning consistently. Despite being annoyed every time that I lost, it was a lot more fun to play a competitive game than to win by default. Now, each time that I see those plastic pieces, I am reminded of warm nights, cold lemonade, and our strategic games of chess.

There are two basic types of motivation. The rewards of extrinsic motivation come from the outside. Fame, money, and power are external motivators. If one simply loves to perform or compete, then one's motivation is more intrinsic. It arises from and rewards within the individual. Can someone be motivated both intrinsically and extrinsically? Certainly! Some people love to make money but also enjoy the risk of trading and investing. Actually, most activities involve varying degrees of both intrinsic and extrinsic motivation.

Studies of writers reveal that they are happiest when they are approaching the end of a manuscript, rather than when they are done. Here's a secret: it's the journey, not the destination, which makes one happy.

For most contestants, the goal is winning. This motivation has both intrinsic and extrinsic elements. Learning to interview, choosing a gown, and getting physically fit are short-term extrinsic goals. In the long run, the process can be a tremendous source of personal growth and intrinsic reward.

Regardless of what drives a contestant, the more that she enjoys the process, the greater her chance of success.

Interview Tip: What made you decide to enter a pageant? Was it a vision of you wearing the crown? The result of encouragement from your friends and family? The factors that motivate you will influence the quality of your performance. Therefore, it is important to understand what inspires you.

23. Give Yourself a Hug

People of high self-esteem are not driven to make themselves superior to others. They do not seek to prove themselves against a comparative statement. Their joy is being who they are, not in being better than someone else.

– Nathaniel Branden, psychotherapist, writer (1930–)

At the beginning of my teaching career, I was deeply involved in the humanistic education. I trained with some of the most renowned leaders in the field. This movement introduced the idea that learning depended on students' perception of themselves, above all other considerations. As a result of this philosophy, students' self-esteem became a priority in the classroom. Every student was supposed to be inculcated with a sense of personal importance. Parents praised children. Teachers praised children. Kids grew up thinking that the world revolved around them and that everything they did was good. Yet there was a flaw in this way of thinking and teaching, as reality soon let the air out of overinflated egos.

Self-esteem cannot be created with compliments or by repeating affirmations. Instead, it has to be earned by meeting challenges and overcoming obstacles. Only then can a person's confidence and self-respect grow.

Similarly, having a winning pageant interview depends first on competence. Like any other skill, a contestant must practice until she learns the basics. Having mastered various techniques, she can then move on to the more creative and expressive aspects of interview. As she becomes proficient in the art of interview, her confidence will grow. This is not the result of being told that she is "good;" in fact, the contestant needs honest and instructive feedback to improve her interview. Instead, it is because her competence comes from her preparation.

During the pageant interview, every contestant should primarily strive to express herself. Security comes from self-acceptance, not trying to imitate someone else. The contestant who is comfortable with herself can focus on the questions, rather than worrying about how she is perceived. Self-esteem demands attention. Self-confidence invites it.

At the conclusion of my yoga class, the teacher asks us to take a moment, close our eyes, and appreciate ourselves for the unique individuals that we are. This is good a good practice for everyone. A positive sense of self comes from knowing that each person is totally original. In the vastness of all that is or ever will be, there is only one you.

Interview Tip: Self-worth does not depend on the judges or on anyone else. It arises from deep inside each person.

24. All about Attitude

The only disability in life is a bad attitude.

– Scott Hamilton, Olympic figure skating
gold medalist, sportscaster, cancer
survivor (1958–)

If I were asked to identify the single most important factor in determining happiness, I would answer—without hesitation—attitude. More than money, education, circumstances, events, successes, or failures, attitude has the greatest influence on whether one succeeds. There is an old truism that says it is not what happens to you in life, but how you respond that determines your happiness.

Consider the man who lost his job, failed in business, suffered a nervous breakdown, and endured defeat in his bid for Congress. No one could blame him for having a negative attitude. But, he persevered. He finally succeeded as no one before or since has. In 1861, Abraham Lincoln became President of the United States.

I have a friend who hosts a radio talk show. From the beginning, she was determined to make her show positive, eschewing news, politics, and conflict of any kind. Instead, she shares inspirational quotes, interviews personal development writers, life coaches, and chats with her listeners. She is the opposite of most radio personalities. At first I found her approach to be like putting sugar on ice cream. But, I tried it, adapting a more positive attitude. I had to admit that life became more pleasant.

I am not an advocate of finding reasons to be positive in all things. Some things just stink! But, everyone has a choice about our attitudes. Being positive has many advantages, and it certainly feels a lot better.

So, a quick, sure-fire way to raise the level of an interview—be positive!

- Smile frequently.
- Listen carefully.
- Find something positive to say in each answer.

- Praise other people for their efforts.
- Never criticize or blame other people.
- Convey a sense of happiness through expression, tone, and posture.
- Enjoy the pageant process.

Interview Tip: Pageant interviews are like the weather. Judges like warmth and sunshine. Rain and wind will send them scurrying for shelter.

25. Chutzpah Unplugged

*Staying quiet about your achievements only leads
to being underappreciated and overlooked.*

– *Peggy Klaus, author, communication
and leadership coach*

In the years when Atlantic City hosted the Miss America pageant, all of the contestants posed for photos on the beach. During one publicity shoot, the photographer asked which woman would be willing to jump into the water. Apparently, the sacrifice of carefully applied make-up and impeccably styled hair didn't appeal to any of the contestants, except one. Without any hesitation, she jumped into the sea. The next day, her picture was on the front page of a New York newspaper.

She had chutzpah.

Before he became governor of California, Arnold Schwarzenegger was a world champion body builder, film star, and real estate magnate. As a teenager, he actually hired a photographer to document his achievements, because he knew that he was going to be a celebrity. Thus, one could say that Governor Schwarzenegger's rise to fame, fortune, and importance was no accident.

He had chutzpah.

Chutzpah is a Yiddish word, and like many Yiddish words, it is difficult to offer an exact translation. Its meanings can include the words audacious, brazen, arrogant, sassy, and supercilious. I prefer to think of chutzpah in less harsh terms—something along the lines of assertiveness, audacity, swagger, or attitude.

When she was preparing for the state pageant, Sara watched several interview tapes of former winners. Although each interview was quite different, she noticed that all the winners had one thing in common. Each woman appeared to be extremely confident and self-assured. As Sara observed, winners have an unshakable sense of self-empowerment. Everything they do is predicated on the belief that they will win. This, however, is not to be confused with arrogance. Conceit,

49

self-importance, and superiority are actually manifestations of insecurity.

The contestant who has chutzpah will not wait for the judges to ask her a question. Instead, she will use the question as a demarcation point for her narrative. She will not be constrained by fear of making a mistake or taking a risk. Nor will she be intimidated by other contestants.

The contestant who has chutzpah acts as though she has already won—the competition is a mere formality that is fun. She can live in the present because she is not held back by personal baggage.

The contestant who has chutzpah seizes the moment. If something goes wrong, she will turn it in her favor.

Interview Tip: The judges won't know about you if you don't tell them.

26. Shooters and Slashers

You've gotta be you because everybody else is taken.

– Geno Auriemma, basketball coach
(1954–)

Coach Auriemma was talking about the guards on his basketball team. He described some as "slashers," who could cut to the basket. Others were pure "shooters," able to sink a 3-point shot from the perimeter. When a slasher wanted to be a shooter or a shooter wanted to be a slasher, it never worked.

Similarly, a contestant's personal style of speaking will emerge with practice. Her speaking style should directly reflect her personality. If she is extroverted, her speech pattern will be rapid, energetic, and physically expressive. On the other hand, if she is more reflective, her pacing might be slower and less vivacious. No style is better than any other. Language, voice, volume, tenor, and pace are a reflection of the individual. Beyond anything else, the contestant should strive to be authentic and personal. Her style should be a direct expression of who she is.

Speakers must also adapt their style to audience size, makeup, and setting. Interview contestants often make the mistake of responding to answers as if they were speaking to a crowd, rather than to an intimate group. That is why they appear to be making a speech. As a result, the judges feel detached and distant from them. Others sound as though they are reading from a teleprompter; their word choice is more consistent with written instead of spoken language. The result is an interview style that is contrived and stiff.

Instead, the intimacy of the pageant interview is suited to a conversational style. A contestant should speak to the judges as though she is talking to her best friend's mother, in her kitchen. Her feelings should infuse her answers with energy and life. And remember, the pageant judge has a short period of time to get to know the contestant. The intimate nature of the pageant interview lends itself to a very personal style of expression.

Judges don't always remember what contestants say as much as how they make them feel, so it is equally important to convey sincerity. This can be accomplished by speaking candidly and expressing genuine feelings. To do this, the contestant must find out if she is a shooter or a slasher, and then make the most of her style.

Interview Tip: Successful speakers are comfortable being themselves.

27. Friendly Persuasion

The real art of conversation is not only to say the right thing at the right place but to leave unsaid the wrong thing at the tempting moment.

– Lady Dorothy Nevill, writer, hostess, horticulturist (1826–1913)

Many years ago, I participated in an enlightening experiment that compared one-way and two-way communication. Each of us was paired with another person, who was told to give instructions for solving a problem. The second person was not allowed to ask for feedback or communicate in any way. The experiment was repeated, only during the second time, questions were allowed. Which method do you think worked most efficiently?

Communication with little or no feedback, like a pageant interview, is difficult. Each judge asks a question, and the contestant responds. It is essentially one-way communication. As previously discussed, the usual response is a monologue. Thus, the contestant often sounds like she is making a speech, which is disconnected from the judges.

Instead, a good interview should sound and feel like a conversation. It has continuity, flow, and spontaneity. There is no self-consciousness or sense of scripting. Although there is very little give and take, the contestant can overcome this situation by knowing what she wants to say and speaking to each judge as if he or she were a friend of her family. At the same time, the contestant must remember to be respectful and deferential to the judges' status. Most judges will have a subtle response to a contestant's answer. However, the one-way communication makes it difficult to read those responses with any degree of accuracy.

The pageant interview is about friendly persuasion, cajoling and convincing the judges that the interviewee is the best candidate. Answers that are in a conversational tone and manner are the best way to win over the judges. A conversation is

53

- spontaneous and expressive,
- continuous and flowing,
- energetic and friendly,
- persuasive and positive,
- spoken in everyday language, and
- polite and playful.

Interview Tip: Speak the way you would to a respected family friend.

II. THE ART AND SCIENCE OF INTERVIEW

28. Do Your Homework

All things are difficult before they are easy.

– Thomas Fuller, Clergyperson,
Author (1608–1661)

You can't talk about what you don't know. Saying something substantive will be one of the ways the judges separate the contestants. The pageant contestant—whether local, state, or national—should have a wide range of knowledge. Some contestants feel that it is futile to study, since they can't be experts on everything. Yet one can become a generalist. Learn a little bit about a lot of different things. Develop a few talking points for each. This is a pageant interview, not Meet the Press.

Begin by brainstorming questions. Brainstorming is a lateral thinking technique for generating ideas. Just write anything down that comes to mind, without judgment or censorship. The objective is quantity, not quality. The contestant should add a question anytime that she gets an idea or hears something interesting. In no time, the number of questions generated will be surprising. Doing this will stimulate thinking.

There are certain questions that, in all probability, will be encountered by all contestants. As a judge, I have been bewildered by the obvious fact that many contestants did not prepare for predictable questions: "Why do you want to be Miss _____?" "Why should we select you as Miss _____?" "What is your favorite book and why?"

While brainstorming questions, a contestant could also talk to women who have been in pageants to find out the kinds of questions that they were asked. This is not to suggest that a contestant can or should try to anticipate all of the questions that the judges might ask. However, by preparing for obvious questions, a contestant can feel more competent and ready.

The next phase of preparation involves gathering information. Read newspapers and magazines, listen to the evening news, and check out the Internet. I have given some contestants subscriptions to Psychology

Today. Regularly read the editorial pages of several papers to experience opposing points of view. A contestant should consider these comments within the context of her own thoughts and feelings. These will teach a contestant to think critically. Magazines like Time and Newsweek also present thoughtful analyses of contemporary issues.

Put down the iPod and the cell phone and begin to tune in to information!

Interview Tip: Knowing the right question will help you find the right answer.

29. The Mock Interview

Take advantage of every opportunity to practice your
communication skills so that when important occasions arise
you will have the gift, the style, the sharpness, the clarity,
and the emotions to affect other people.

– Jim Rohn, entrepreneur, author,
motivational speaker (1930–2009)

There was a famous Navy admiral who was known for "testing"
junior officers by making them wait —sometimes for days—for an interview
with him. Similarly, in business, the "stress interview" is intended to exhaust
and frustrate a potential employee. These interviews can include panels
of questioners and go on for 6 hours or more. By contrast, the pageant
interview is a friendly environment. The judges want the contestant to
succeed; thus, they usually adapt their questions to the individual.

Most women prepare for the pageant interview by participating
in a series of mock interviews. The panel usually consists of people who
have some relationship to the pageant. Most mock interviews use the same
questions. Criticism is limited to the content of answers, with an occasional
reference to posture or the color of the contestant's business suit.

The problem with mock interviews is that the feedback is
subjective, and contradictory information is often given to the contestant.
Further, practicing the same way by doing the same thing over and over
reinforces the same behaviors. To improve, the contestant must understand the concept, skills, and nuances of an effective interview. One of
the best ways to learn this is by modeling good interviews.

I was asked to be on a mock interview panel for a woman who was
visiting from the South. There, it was anticipated that she would be the
next state titleholder. After the first round of questioning, the rather large,
experienced panel offered absolutely nothing critical. The second round
brought a similar response. Finally, I broke the precedent by pointing out
that "dead air" followed each of her answers. A silent space, before the
judges pose the next question, can be indicative of a problem. Questions

that flow smoothly from one to another indicate energy and interest by the judges.

My comment was like taking the cork out of a bottle. The formerly reticent panel bubbled to life. They began to offer a level of criticism that I am sure surprised, but ultimately helped, the contestant. Later, her mother, who was a professor at a prestigious law school, thanked me.

Mock interviews are a valuable part of pageant preparation. The panel should consist of persons who have knowledge and experience in many disparate fields. I recruit several media personalities, such as news anchors and broadcasters, for mock interviews. These professionals can provide valuable insight into a contestant's presentation.

As much as possible, the mock interview should simulate the actual interview. Questions should cover a gamut of subjects. While I favor immediate feedback following each round of questions, the contestant and her interview coach need to talk about the panel's suggestions and decide what to incorporate and what to ignore.

The bottom line is that a contestant needs to experience a variety of teaching methods, not the least of which is the mock interview.

Interview Tip: If the mock interview is challenging, then the pageant interview will be easy.

30. Leaving Your Comfort Zone

Move out of your comfort zone. You can only grow
if you are willing to feel awkward and uncomfortable when
you try something new.

– Brian Tracy, self-help author (1944–)

My first formal experience with presentation skills was totally unanticipated. In 1987, I co-wrote an educational unit about advertising art. It won a Celebration of Excellence Award from the State of Connecticut Department of Education. The award required that all recipients attend a 1-week training session during the summer.

A small group of us were selected to have our lesson videotaped during this training session. As an experienced teacher, I was used to speaking to a classroom filled with students. Yet, the prospect of being videotaped intimidated me. Plus, the school where we met was not air-conditioned. The day of my presentation, I don't think an inch of my shirt was dry. But I made myself leave my comfort zone and never looked back.

Most certainly, change can be uncomfortable. There is a fear of what might be ahead, the fear of having made the wrong choice, and the fear of failure. All of these hold people back. Leaving what is familiar and safe requires courage and faith.

Moving outside of the comfort zone, which is sometimes known as "pushing the envelope," inevitably produces anxiety. Think about how much angst a simple thing like changing one's hairstyle causes. To avoid the stress that comes with confronting change, people procrastinate, rationalize, and otherwise make excuses for their inaction. This is self-defeating behavior for a woman who is preparing for a pageant.

As I have previously stated, practicing the same type of questions with a familiar panel will not produce the kind of challenges that will raise the contestant to the next level. She must move out of her comfort zone. Panelists need to ramp up both the difficulty of questions and the stress level of mock interviews. Informed feedback is a necessity.

The mock interview is the place to learn from mistakes. By the time the pageant comes, the contestant should have encountered every contingency that may occur during the interview. The result will be a contestant who is confident in her ability to handle any question.

As a contestant's comfort zone expands, her versatility and choices grow exponentially. Resist, and her comfort zone will eventually become a prison that confines her to what has been and locks out what she can become.

Interview Tip: Leave your comfort zone by simulating the conditions of the actual pageant interview. Ask mock judges for challenging questions, and welcome critical feedback.

31. Mixed Messages

> If you don't know where you are going, you will
> probably end up somewhere else.
>
> – *Laurence J. Peter, educator, writer*
> *(1919–1988)*

There is an urban myth about a pageant contestant who was asked, "What do you see yourself doing in 10 years?" She answered, "I would like to be a brain surgeon or a nail technician." OK! Before any nail techs go ballistic, there is absolutely nothing wrong with that line of work. However, there is a chasm—wider than the Grand Canyon—between operating on a brain and filing a broken fingernail.

This is a classic example of a mixed message. It contains verbal or nonverbal information that is contradictory. Such mixed messages can erode a contestant's credibility beyond redemption.

Incongruous messages are common during pageant interviews. The contestant who describes herself as "energetic and enthusiastic," in a plodding, low voice while she leans on the podium for support, gives a mixed message. Even the pageant itself contains contradictory messages. The swimsuit competition is called "fitness," but I have known swimsuit winners who have never seen the inside of a gym. Fitness is a measure of work. It can't be assessed visually. All of this aside, the interview contestant needs to be consistent with her answers and nonverbal cues. Conflicting messages are usually interpreted as being false.

There are several ways that contestants send mixed messages. The most obvious is by what she says. Making statements like, "I don't read books but I like to read," are conflicting. Judges will respond to these, whether they are consciously aware of it or not. For example, if a contestant's arms hug her hips as she explains, "I'm a free spirit," there will be a perceived incongruity. Energy level, as expressed through the volume and tone of voice, should be consistent with the contestant's answers. Describing oneself as "a people person," without making eye contact, will leave the judges wondering. The statement "I am a strong leader," spoken in a voice that is barely audible is yet another mixed message. A contestant must make certain that her message, both verbal and nonverbal, is convincing and consistent.

Most mixed messages occur because the contestant is trying to represent herself as something she is not. Thinking that the judges are looking for a certain answer or personal quality, the contestant gives a disingenuous answer. The best way to be is honest. The conflict that gives rise to mixed messages will disappear, like smoke in the air, when the contestant is genuine.

Interview Tip: Words, expression, tone, voice, and body language need to be congruent.

32. Feeling the Squeeze

How are expectations and attitude related?
If you expect to win and don't, you will consider yourself
as less than you are. If you expect to lose, you will never win.
If your attitude is that you expect to have a good time, do
your best to learn new things, have a new experience,
and make new friends, you will always be a winner.

– John Eliot, author (1972–)

At one pageant, while the contestants waited for the finalists to be announced, each was asked the same question, "How do you respond to pressure?" I sat in the audience hoping Cherie would remember the last quote that I had sent her. It was from the great tennis player, Billie Jean King, who said, "Pressure is a privilege." Cherie had swept the local pageant. At the state level, however, the competition was greater.

Pressure can make some contestants crazy. It robs them of reason and makes them act on impulse. Stories of sabotaged gowns and other acts of pageant vandalism are ubiquitous. The mind interprets the pressure of a pageant as a threat. It reacts by activating the "fight or flight" response in the brain. The rush of adrenaline that increases heart rate and breathing and makes one perspire is simply a sign that one is ready to compete.

No matter how bright or talented, the way a contestant responds to pressure will be a determining factor in the outcome of a pageant. A contestant can use the pressure of competition to raise the level of her performance or allow it to be as constrictive as a dress that is three sizes too small. It is best that she allows the other competitors to inspire rather than to threaten her. After all, striving to be her personal best should be her ultimate goal.

Although competition can elevate performance, keep the pageant in the perspective—wanting to win too badly will disrupt anyone's best efforts.

Interview Tip: Allow the spirit of competition to bring about your best performance

DID I REALLY SAY THAT?

33. Critics and Criticism

The only people who never fail are those who never try.

– Ilka Chase, author, actress, humorist
(1905–1978)

The world is filled with critics. It seems that everyone has the answer for everyone else. One can pick up the editorial page of any newspaper and read how the government, religion, and politics would be perfect if only the world followed the dictates of some pundit. It is far easier to demonize those with whom we disagree than to offer constructive solutions to challenges.

Many years ago, I wrote a book about the creative process. Among the dozens of rejection letters I received from publishers, one letter was personal. This letter was extremely critical and detailed. I didn't like it, but I had to admit that the writer made some valid points. The critique made my work better.

Kelly was one of the best students whom I ever taught. She was an extraordinary combination of aptitude, attitude, and self-motivation. In January, one of the town's most respected police officers was killed during a standoff. Late in the spring, the superintendent called me. He wanted the school system to donate a piece of artwork in the officer's honor to the public safety facility that was being built. I suggested that a portrait of the officer could be painted by one of our students. The previous fall, Kelly had won a gold key in a statewide art competition for her self-portrait. We asked Kelly if she would be interested, and she accepted the challenge without hesitation.

Within a week, she had painted a credible portrait. For the next 3 months, she worked days and weekends, perfecting her artwork. On Monday, she would bring the painting to us for constructive criticism. Every time she reworked one thing, we found something else that needed attention. She remained unflappable. The day the painting was to be presented to the officer's widow, Kelly retouched it for 3 hours, under our watchful eyes. The portrait was magnificent. It was a wonderful tribute to a fallen hero and an expression of Kelly's talent and tenacity.

Yet perhaps Kelly's greatest gift was the ability to absorb critical feedback—without being defensive or indignant—and use it to improve her work. This is one of the secrets of personal growth.

Being told how well she was interviewing was not making Amanda's interview better. To improve, a contestant must deal with increasing levels of difficulty. I warned Amanda that the next mock interview would test her limits. I instructed the judges to ask her the most difficult questions, as I wanted her to experience stress. To my delight, Amanda welcomed the challenge because she knew it would make her better.

A contestant must try not to label criticism as negative or positive. Instead, she should think of it as information. People become defensive when they feel that criticism is personal or unfair. Remember that constructive criticism is not a personal attack. Responding to feedback with rationalizations or excuses defeats its purpose.

There is a caveat, though. Not all criticism is constructive. Few people are aware of the nuances of an interview. Many contestants are given erroneous or contradictory advice. Do what feels right.

Interview Tip: Listen to everyone, but don't do what everyone says.

34. Grace under Fire

The truest mark of being born with great qualities
is being born without envy.

– François de La Rochefoucauld, author
(1613–1680)

The young woman waited anxiously, along with five other finalists. She was a nurse, attractive and well spoken. When it was announced that she was the third runner-up, the disappointment immediately registered on her face. Still, she accepted the rather large trophy and stood by as the winner was crowned. Meanwhile, anger boiled inside her until it could no longer be contained. Without any warning, she smashed the trophy to the floor, shattering it. Then, she stormed off of the stage in tears.

Because one doesn't agree with a decision doesn't mean that it is the wrong decision. The judges have a difficult job. They do their best. Yes, sometimes judges do make questionable calls; sometimes everyone makes bad calls. However, before a contestant criticizes, she must think about the long-term effect of her words on others and on herself.

The fastest way that a contestant can undo all of her hard work is to have a tantrum onstage. How do you think the audience will remember the contestant described in this section? Every pageant contestant leaves a legacy. The contestant who behaves with grace will be admired. Additionally, if she intends to compete in the future, it is advantageous to leave a positive impression with the pageant officials and judges.

As a pageant competitor and, more importantly, a person graced with poise, the pageant presents a wonderful opportunity for personal growth. Here are some ways a contestant can do so:

- congratulate each competitor,
- thank the judges,
- write a thank-you note to the pageant directors,
- celebrate her effort and appreciate how fortunate she is,
- do not make excuses or place blame,
- share in the joy of others,

• respect herself and honor other people, and
• learn from the experience.

Interview Tip: The remedy for disappointment is gratitude.

35. More than Mascara

One of the most wonderful things in nature is a glance of the eye; it transcends speech; it is the bodily symbol of identity.

– Ralph Waldo Emerson, poet, essayist,
philosopher (1803–1882)

Eyes have been celebrated in art, literature, song, and poetry for thousands of years. A few better known phrases include "eyes are the window of the soul," "a sight for sore eyes," "the apple of my eye," and "beauty is in the eye of the beholder." Marketing researchers measure pupil dilation as an indication of how people respond to a product. Further, public speakers, politicians, and salespeople use their eyes to establish a relationship with audiences, constituents, and customers.

Making eye contact is vital for an interview contestant. The eyes reach out as surely as an extended hand. That said, eye contact can be tricky. How a person looks at another is the first step in establishing a relationship. Staring at the judges too long can be interpreted as threatening. Also, refusing to make eye contact can be taken as a sign of arrogance or dishonesty.

The rules of eye contact are subtle. The interview contestant should look at the person who is asking the question. Make eye contact with all of the judges when answering a question. Typically, listeners glance at the contestant from 1 to 7 seconds about 75% of the time. Contestants are usually advised to make eye contact from 2 to 4 seconds, but don't try to count seconds. It will be a distraction. When a contestant pauses to think or to choose the proper word, she will look to the right or left, depending on which hemisphere of the brain is dominant.

Eye contact can reduce the perception of distance by half. Skilled public speakers will briefly look directly at their audience each time that they want to emphasize a point. They also sweep the crowd, meeting the eyes of their audience with a brief glance.

Eye contact should not be contrived. The contestant should use her eyes to make a connection with the judges. Therefore, she should

remember to

- establish eye contact from the moment that she is introduced,
- initially make eye contact with each judge,
- look at the whole face and don't stare,
- break eye contact occasionally by looking away,
- make eye contact with the judge who is asking the question,
- look at all of the judges during her answer,
- alternate her focus on a person's left eye and then his or her right eye, and
- let her eyes "smile."

Interview Tip: Use your eyes to make each judge feel as though you are having a conversation with him or her.

36. Listening Speaks Softly

Listening, not imitation, may be the sincerest form of flattery.

– *Dr. Joyce Brothers, psychologist, advice
columnist (1927–)*

Her impact was immediate and profound. She was smart, beautiful, and carried a gun. She gave kids her cell phone number, so they could call her if they were in trouble. She was as much a counselor as an authority figure. Ciara was our school resource officer; a disciplined policewoman and a friend to students and faculty. What most people didn't know was that Ciara was also a gifted poet who had a degree in literature.

Back then, she was the only person whom I would allow to hear my poetry. I would come to her office with what I had written. She would put her face in her palms, as thought she were praying, and give me her undivided attention. She died much too soon, the victim of a senseless act of violence. I write poetry—to a great extent—because of her. Ciara's everlasting gift was that she listened to me.

In this culture, we think of communication as being active. We assert a point of view, make speeches, and engage in debates. Thoughts spin in our minds before the other person has finished talking. Retorts are prepackaged, like frozen food. Interrupting is common.

Listening validates people. It communicates interest and respect. To ensure that the message spoken is the message heard, psychologists use a technique called "active listening." The active listener repeats the essence of what was said back to the speaker. If the interpretation has not been heard as it was intended, the speaker can immediately correct it. While I am not an advocate of repeating the question, listening to it is extremely important.

Many interview contestants are too quick on the trigger. Before the judge has finished asking a question, her answer begins. Meanwhile, her brain has been racing to prepare a response. This is the reason a contestant gives an answer that has little to do with the question. Interrupting a judge's question is disrespectful. The contestant runs the

71

risk of not hearing the full question, and she appears to be tense.

Listening is a manifestation of mindfulness. A contestant should try to empty her mind by focusing on the question. In turn, listening will help calm the contestant by directing her consciousness outside of herself. Good listeners are as rare as roses in the snow.

Interview Tip: Listen intently until you are certain the judge has completed asking the question.

37. Bubbles in Space

Each organism, no matter how simple or complex,
has around it a sacred bubble of space, a bit of mobile
territoriality which only a few other organisms are allowed
to penetrate and then only for short periods of time.

– Edward T. Hall, anthropologist
(1914–2009)

Gretchen's shoes tapped audibly as she rapidly walked to the podium. Taking a step toward the judges, she said, "How do you like our New England weather?" Her tone was abrasive, and the volume of her voice was loud. The question was peculiar, since all of the judges lived in the area. Her arms thrashed the air aggressively, and the forward step she took brought her nearer to the judges' table. All six judges, who had been sitting upright in their chairs, leaned backward, every time she spoke. It was as though someone with bad breath had come too close. She had invaded the judge's space.

When I was in high school, I read a groundbreaking book, The Hidden Dimension, by cultural anthropologist Edward T. Hall. The book examined how people use personal space to communicate. He called this "proxemics." It's as if each of us lives in a clear bubble that surrounds our bodies. We consider that bubble space to be our own. Unconsciously, people maintain personal space with uncanny accuracy, adjusting it to within a fraction of an inch. If someone invades that space, by coming too close, we feel uncomfortable or even threatened.

The use of space is a product of culture. How close you stand to a person is also determined by relationship. According to Dr. Hall, the conversational distance for friends and family is about 10 inches. For acquaintances and people whom we do not know well, casual personal distance is 4–12 feet. Public speaking distance is 12–25 feet. Women tend to lean in during conversation and bring themselves physically closer during conversation than men do. The interview contestant may find that she is somewhere in between.

The way a contestant structures space during an interview will have an unconscious influence on the judges' perception. I refer to the area between the judges and contestant as "affective space." One of the contestant's goals is to invite the judges into her affective space. This doesn't mean that she says, "Hey judges, do you want to move closer?" It is the perception of space rather than the actual distance. Even if the judges are 8 feet away, the perception of that distance can be halved by the contestant. Many times, I have observed judges leaning toward a candidate with whom they felt comfortable.

Now, don't be discouraged if the judges maintain their initial posture. Leaning in is just one indicator of shortened affective distance. The most effective way to make space open and inviting is to maintain a friendly, conversational tone and open body language. The unspoken signals that a contestant gives to the judges will register at an unconscious level.

Stepping to one side of the podium, if permitted, is a way to close the affective distance. Avoid pointing or moving toward the judges' table. Laughter is like putting out a Welcome! sign. Understanding how to reach out to the judges without invading their space will add another dimension to a contestant's interview.

Interview Tip: Treat the judges as though they are within your personal space.

38. First Impressions: The Secret Weapon of Interviews

The answer is that we are not helpless in the face
of our first impressions. They may bubble up from the
unconscious—from behind a locked door inside of our
brain—but just because something is outside of
awareness doesn't mean it's outside of control.

– Malcolm Gladwell, author (1963–)

In his book, Blink: The Power of Thinking without Thinking, Malcolm Gladwell makes the compelling argument for the reliability of first impressions. Using what he calls "thin slicing" of behavior, people can make better instant judgments by focusing on relevant facts than by using a more rational approach to problem solving. He illustrates his point with stories about art forgeries, emergency room triage, marital fidelity, and even speed dating.

In one experiment, people were asked to remember items on a list. Subjects tended to recall the first and last items, with the first few being remembered the best. This is known as the "primacy effect." In other words, the first impression the contestant makes on the judges is the most likely to be remembered. During the first 2-7 seconds of an interview, the contestant will be carefully scrutinized. First impressions remain long after the contestant has left the room.

Anna asked me if it was true that the judges can tell a lot about a contestant by the way she enters the room. It is true! Laura Naumann, an assistant psychology professor at Sonoma State University, found that simply by observing full-body photos, the average person can perceive at least four personality traits—likability, extroversion, openness to new experiences, and self-esteem.

The first thing the judges see is the way a contestant moves. They will respond to her posture, carriage, and walk. Her stride should convey a sense of confidence and energy. She should look toward the judges as she enters the room. She should also smile as though she is happy, even if she is scared.

Before a contestant greets them, she must turn toward the judges and stop. This is important. Sometimes, contestants rush and begin talking while they are still moving. Remember, first words set the tone for the entire interview.

Take a page from a football coach's playbook. The first few plays are scripted because the players will be too excited to think about what to do. Likewise, a contestant's salutation should be decided prior to the interview. The greeting should show deference to the judges. Avoid using slang acknowledgments such as "Hi!", "Hey!", "What's up?", or "How ya doing?" Standard salutations, like "Good morning," "Good afternoon," and "Nice to meet you" are more appropriate. Be creative, but don't try to be cute or clever.

The intonation and inflection of a contestant's voice should say, "I am happy to be here and can't wait to get started." A contestant should practice entering the room and making her introduction until she is self-assured and poised. Then, she should close the interview by telling the judges that she enjoyed the interview. Thank them for their attention and wish them a good day, or something similar.

First impressions are cast in concrete, so a contestant must make sure that her imprint is deep enough to last when she leaves the room.

Interview Tip: Prepare and practice your greeting until it appears that you haven't prepared.

39. First Steps

If you're walking down the right path and you're willing to keep walking, eventually you'll make progress.

– Barak Obama, senator, U. S. President (1961–)

Watching Judy walk in her evening gown was excruciating. She moved like a zombie in a B movie. Her entire body was stiff and immobile, as though she were in pain. Somehow, she had developed the idea that a contestant should move in slow motion.

As discussed previously, the first thing that the judges will see is the contestant's entrance. Before she utters a word, the familiar act of walking will have a significant, subliminal influence on the judges' assessment .

Experiments have shown how minor changes in attitude can influence even a physical process as automatic as walking. Elderly people, exposed to words associated with positive aging, walked 9% faster than those who were not similarly primed. Depressed people take shorter steps and move more slowly than people who are joyful. Stride length, speed, arm swing, and footfall can be correlated with emotions, like happiness, pride, and anger.

Walking does not have to be entirely unconscious. Understanding the relationship between movement and emotion will help the contestant take those first important steps toward winning the crown. If a contestant is feeling anxious, this emotion will be manifested in her walk. Conversely, if she is filled with excitement about her interview and can't wait for it to start, her walk will convey an entirely different message.

A contestant should remember the following:

- Posture. Stand up straight, with her head, shoulders, and hips in line.
- Arms. Allow her arms to swing freely in rhythm with her strides.
- Speed. Walk briskly, but don't break into a trot.
- Stride length. Control her speed by increasing the number, not the length, of steps.

- Foot strike. Try to be light on her feet to minimize heel tap.
- Eye line. Look straight ahead or at the judges.
- Chin. Keep her chin parallel to the ground—don't look down.

Interview Tip: To establish good posture, shrug your shoulders once, then let them drop into a comfortable position.

40. Poetry in Motion

Well-crafted body language helps people in all areas
of their career, particularly in interview situations where
first impressions are crucial.

– Campbell Sallabank, CEO

The contestant's hands looked as though they were glued to her hips. The news anchor made sweeping gestures directly in the eye line of the viewer. The meteorologist rubbed his hands together, as if he were washing them. The body language of these people was a manifestation of their internal state. In each case, it detracted from their performance.

When a person's speaks, words are not the only way he or she is communicating. Body language is an amalgamation of posture, eye contact, gesture, movement, voice, and expression. Estimates on the amount of information communicated through body language range from 55% to 93%. The latter seems excessive, but nonverbal communication is certainly significant.

In his book, The Political Brain, Drew Weston cites an experiment conducted by psychologists Nalini Ambady and Robert Rosenthal that demonstrates the importance of nonverbal communication. Observers watched 30-second video clips, without audio, of university teachers at the beginning of one semester. Observers, looking solely at the teachers' body language, were able to predict end-of-term student evaluations of these teachers with phenomenal accuracy. The same teachers who were initially rated highly based on a short nonverbal video clip were rated as the better teachers months later.

As a judge, one of the things I look for is consistency between spoken message and body language. More than once, I have heard a woman say she was open and friendly, while her arms were folded across her chest and her face was contorted into a scowl. Bodily cues are among the most reliable nonverbal signals because people generally have less conscious control over them.

A contestant must become aware of the nonverbal messages

that she is sending. They will change as she becomes more proficient, confident, and relaxed.

Interview Tip: To learn about body language, try watching a TV show or a movie without sound. Then study tapes of your interview without sound. Try to analyze the messages that you are conveying nonverbally.

41. Visions of Sugar Plums

Peak performers develop powerful mental images
of the behavior that will lead to the desired results.
They see in their mind's eye the result they want,
and the actions leading to it.

– Charles Garfield, author, motivational
speaker, professor

I was preparing for a team triathlon when Diana, a classically trained opera singer, invited me to hear her performance in The Mikado. I had been her business manager during the state pageant. By the second hour of her performance, my mind was on other things. I was mentally competing in the triathlon, even though my body was firmly planted in a rather uncomfortable theater seat. I pictured myself on my bicycle, pedaling hard over the hills and then slicing across the water in our racing canoe. My pulse increased, and I felt myself begin to sweat.

Recall the lines from "The Night Before Christmas" that went, "The children were nestled all sung in their beds,/While visions of sugar plums danced in their heads?" Likewise, mental imagery can be just as vivid for adults as it was when we were children. Research shows that going through the motions mentally can enhance performance as well— and sometimes better—than physical practice. This is because mental rehearsal activates more abstract neural representations of physical skill. Of course, complicated activities that rely on sensory feedback still require physical practice.

I have written articles, presented workshops, and conducted dozens of guided imagery exercises. Participants always describe the sensations and experiences as real. Such mental imagery exercises are used in medicine, athletic training, and creative arts.

For the contestant, visualization should be an integral part of her pageant preparation. The most productive time to do a mental rehearsal is just before falling asleep. This is called the hypnogogic state of imagery, when the mind is most receptive to suggestion. It is important that she be

81

specific and methodical in developing the image. She must pay attention to every detail, be conscious of how she feels emotionally, and remember the tactile sensations that she experiences. Her heart will beat faster, and she will hear the audience applaud. With enough rehearsal, a contestant's body will develop an automatic response to what she has rehearsed in her mind. Visualization is a kind of self-hypnosis. I always tell a contestant to suggest mentally how she wants to feel and to rehearse what she wants to do—then, it will become a reality.

Interview Tip: Visualization is like watching a DVD. Practice visualization by trying to feel each movement as though you were actually doing it. When you begin, go through the activity slowly, focusing on details. As you become more competent, practice in real time.

42. Stopping Time

The most precious things in speech are pauses.

– *Sir Ralph David Richardson, actor*
(1902–1983)

Whenever I give a formal speech, I begin by standing at the podium. I scan the audience for quite a while without saying a word. This gives me time to settle down and make eye contact with the audience. If people are talking, I wait for them to stop. It's an old teacher trick. By then, the audience is wondering what's going on. They are ready to listen or watch me have a heart attack. Either way, I have their attention. This is a "pregnant pause," a term derived from Michelangelo's Sistine Chapel fresco in which Adam is just about to touch the hand of God. It is a supercharged moment just before an action occurs. There is a sense that time is suspended for just an instant.

I have discussed the use of pauses to replace verbal hitches. Skilled speakers use the pause for other purposes as well. A pause is an opportunity for the contestant to gather her thoughts and to gain composure. As I said previously, many interview contestants answer questions too quickly. Pausing before giving an answer implies that the contestant is introspective. It also counteracts the idea that answers are packaged or rehearsed. A pause can be used as punctuation; a brief pause at the conclusion of a sentence is like a period at the end of a sentence.

Experiments have shown that phrases containing pauses were retained more accurately than those without pauses. Pausing after making an important point increases dramatic effect. During that momentary void, the listener's brain is actually digesting the answer.

Also, everyone has the tendency to talk too fast when nervous. A pause will put the brakes on a rapid-fire delivery.

A few precautions need to be considered. A contestant shouldn't conclude her answers with a pause. In this situation, the pause indicates that there is more to come. Instead, the content and inflection of her voice should indicate that she has finished answering.

Too often, I have watched contestants take long pauses (more than 10 seconds), which drive me crazy. They are deadly to the interview. Later in this book, I will discuss what to do if a contestant doesn't know the answer to a question. Regardless, a lengthy pause is to be avoided. Don't overuse pauses, either. Pauses are like condiments on food. Applied judiciously, they bring out flavor. Overdone, they spoil the meal.

Interview Tip: Practice pausing by reading an article aloud, inserting pauses where you think they will help convey meaning. Also, assign yourself a predetermined number of pauses during a mock interview. A pause that is too long makes the contestant appear like a deer in headlights. Keep the pauses short and intermittent.

43. Perspiration on a Butterfly's Wings

There are only two types of speakers in the world:
(1) the nervous, and (2) liars.

– Mark Twain (Samuel Clemens),
author, humorist (1835–1910)

The symptoms are familiar: shaking hands, dry mouth, perspiration, nausea, and hyperventilation. There is the sense that death may occur at any moment and would, in fact, be preferable.

Everyone gets nervous. Even seasoned performers can be victims of paralyzing stage freight. At a 1967 concert in Central Park, Barbra Streisand forgot the words to several songs. This incident triggered a phobia that kept her from singing in public for 27 years. Oscar-winning actress Kim Basinger attributed her anxiety to childhood fears associated with reading aloud in class. Considered the greatest Shakespearean actor of all time, Sir Laurence Oliver's fear of forgetting his lines kept him from the stage for 5 years.

Fear and anticipation release butterflies in our stomachs and put a boa constrictor around our throats. The inner voice spins a scenario of all the ways that we can disappoint and embarrass ourselves. The mind is filled with "what if...?" scenarios. Extreme nervousness makes it difficult to focus; the brain goes blank, hands shake, and the heart pounds so hard that one imagines that people can see it. Sometimes, perspiration makes an unwelcome appearance. We begin to feel weak and vulnerable. Negative thinking chips away at confidence faster than a sculptor with a jackhammer.

Nervousness is a biological response to the fear of losing control. When a perceived threat is nonphysical, all that nervous energy is turned inward. Understanding that there is no threat and that there are ways to deal with being nervous neutralizes the natural "fight or flight" response. For me, the feeling of being nervous has always been worse than anything that ever did or ever could happen.

There is a bright side to being nervous. Anxiety—up to a certain point—provides a physical and mental edge. Beyond that point, it can paralyze the unfortunate performer. In a study at Harvard University, students taking the Graduate Record Exam were told that their nervousness was positive and would improve their performance. Subsequently, they did consistently better than students who were told nothing.

Reappraising nervous energy can have a positive effect on performance. Before I give a speech, I still like to feel a bit anxious. Not only does this improve my delivery, it tells me that I am invested in the outcome. A little nervousness goes a long way.

With practice, the contestant can learn how to use nervous energy to infuse energy into her interview.

Interview Tip: Most of us try to suppress pre-competition nerves. Instead of fighting against yourself, go with the flow of energy. Reframe your response by understanding that being anxious is a natural response to the situation. Used properly, that nervous energy can raise the level of your performance.

44. How to Tame a Bumblebee

I get nervous when I don't get nervous. If I'm nervous,
I know I'm going to have a good show.

*– Beyoncé Knowles, singer, songwriter,
actress (1981–)*

It must have been on my grocery basket when I picked it up. I felt something soft and furry on my fingers. Looking down, there it was—a bumblebee. I calmly watched it crawl along my fingers, feeling the fuzzy hairs brush against my skin. Then, it was gone.

During the course of our lives, many situations will cause anxiety: SAT exams, first dates, second dates, athletic competitions, public speaking, and, of course, interviews. No one is immune to nerves. Having to perform—on a test, in a game, or before an audience—produces an autonomic response. The higher the stakes, the greater the anxiety.

However, anxiety is not necessarily negative. The adrenalin that the nervous system releases into the bloodstream can make a contestant alert and focused. Instead of trying to resist the natural anxiety that precedes an interview, a contestant must learn how to channel that feeling into positive energy.

When she competed in the state pageant, Cindy won the interview award. Since that time, her career path has led her to jobs as a reporter, news anchor, and media relations specialist. At one point, she interviewed for a job as a pharmaceutical salesperson. About midway into her second 4-hour interview, Cindy sensed that the person interviewing her was dissatisfied with her responses. This made her extremely nervous. Yet rather than allowing her emotions to undermind her interview, she became more aggressive with her answers. As it turned out, that was exactly what the company wanted—someone who could respond to rejection assertively. As Cindy demonstrated, being nervous is not synonymous with collapse. Instead, it can energize and elevate performance.

So, let's redefine the anxiety from a negative emotion to positive source of energy. Pre-interview anxiety can bring heightened alertness, sharpened perception, and an energy supply that makes Red Bull look like lemonade. To do so, it is vital that a contestant must remember the following.

Practice. Remember that confidence comes from being fully prepared.

Desensitize. Recognize that repeated exposure will make the interview familiar and less threatening.

Rationalize self-talk. Understand that her fears are unfounded.

Be mindful. Focus on the present moment rather than imagining the future.

Be strong. Appreciate her personal, physical, and mental attributes, especially her courage.

Breathe. Slow the breathing, and make inhalations and exhalations equal in length.

Sing. Silently sing a favorite song, which has a beat that will slow her heart rate.

Focus. Concentrate on the judges, rather than what you are feeling.

Loosen up. Know that mistakes don't matter; there is nothing she can do that can't be fixed.

Smile. Take a 30-second vacation, and imagine a time and place when she felt calm.

Even a bumblebee will calm down if one knows how to act.

Interview Tip: This yoga exercise will help you remain calm. Rub the inside of your wrists together in a circular motion. You will feel the energy, a slight warming, and a sense of composure.

45. Speaking a Foreign Language

Language exerts hidden power, like a moon on the tides.

– Rita Mae Brown, author (1944–)

When I was a junior in high school, our English teacher assigned a term paper. His rules were that there could be no more than five spelling errors and two grammatical mistakes. Mind you, this was well before computers and spell check. I anxiously waited as he returned our papers, carefully folded to preserve privacy. I opened my thesis and read, "Well-Written and Well-Developed: F." I had used semicolons instead of commas. Whoops!

Gina did well in every category until her interview. It was as if she spoke an unintelligible, foreign language. Her voice rose at the end of each statement, and it seemed as though every other word was "like." Unable to translate what she was trying to say, the judges zoned out.

Using proper English and correct grammar is imperative during the pageant interview. Language is important. Contestants must avoid using catch phrases, jargon, and popular expressions. Choose standard English: say "yes" of instead of "yeah." Never say "whatever" or "like" unless actually making a comparison.

Using correct English indicates education and the ability to think coherently. Working on grammar, pronunciation, and vocabulary is not just an academic exercise. Good grammar allows fluency. A large vocabulary gives more options for expressing thoughts and feelings. Further, proper pronunciation is associated with intelligence. A contestant should ensure her best:

English use. Develop an ear for English usage by listening to well-spoken people.

Pronunciation. Speak clearly by articulating each word.

Word selection. Choose the word that best expresses what she is trying to say.

Clear speech. Avoid using slang, jargon, and clichés.

Subject–verb agreement. Be certain that these conform

to standard English.

Analogies and metaphors. Use these to make comparisons or to illustrate a point.

Interview Tip: Improve your vocabulary by trying to learn a new word every day. Use that word until it becomes a regular part of your speech. Remember the biggest word is not always the best. Learn the nuances of meaning.

46. Black Holes of Speech

All the great speakers were bad speakers at first.

– Ralph Waldo Emerson, writer
(1803–1882)

For several years, I was a member and chair of the State of Connecticut Department of Education Committee for the Approval of State Teacher Preparation Programs. (Actually, it took me a few years to learn the full name of this committee.) It was a daunting responsibility. Our decisions influenced whether a university received its professional certification. As a part of the process, university presidents, professors, and school administrators testified before the committee. Usually, despite their prodigious educational credentials, impressive accomplishments, and knowledge, their verbal presentations left me feeling like I had taken a sleeping pill. I would often find my attention drifting after a few minutes of run-on sentences and verbal hitches.

Verbal hitches are the "black holes" of speech. Fillers such as "a, a, a, a...," "ummm...," "like...," and "you know..." are verbal ticks. I have a friend who strings his sentences together by extending the word "a-a-n-n-d-d" into the next phrase, creating one long run-on sentence. Once a listener's attention has been diverted to a verbal hitch that is all he or she hears.

No one knows exactly why people add hitches to their speech. Certainly, their use is unconscious. Probably, it is a way of buying time between thoughts. Once, during a TV interview, I began saying "absolutely" to indicate agreement with the interviewer's observation. Now, there was nothing wrong with the word or its use. The problem was that I used it too many times.

If a contestant uses a verbal crutch, it will require a concerted effort to change the habit. I have fined contestants a nickel every time that they inserted a filler word. Like any habitual behavior, reeducation is an awkward, protracted process. The most effective way to deal with a hitch begins with understanding that every empty space between a word or

91

thought does not need to be filled. A pause or lull is perfectly acceptable. In fact, I teach contestants to pause purposely several times during the interview. This has the dual purpose of giving an extra few seconds to respond and making the judges think that the contestant is a reflective thinker.

Thorough preparation and a healthy dose of practice will help alleviate verbal hitches. Avoid verbal hitches, catch phrases, overused phrases and words, and jargon as if they were angry bees. Like, you know what I'm saying?

Interview Tip: Breathing is way to control hitches. By taking and holding a breath for a second or two, the expulsion of air that accompanies filler sounds is unavailable.

47. Definitely Not!

Education should prepare [the] mind to use its own powers of reason and conception rather than filling it with the accumulated misconceptions of the past.

– *Allen Adler, writer (1916–1964)*

In pageant interviews, certain words are used too frequently when answering questions. Many contestants use word "definitely" more times during a pageant than they will for remainder of their lives. Be aware that is so ubiquitous that it automatically carries a negative connotation.

When the first word response to a question is "definitely," the contestant has established an absolute. "Definitely" and other unconditional terms shade toward the negative pole because they are so dogmatic. A contestant who is mentally flexible and understands nuances is better equipped to deal with diverse people and situations, which is definitely expected for a winner. While it is fine to have opinions, they are subject to change. Further, it is a sign of respect to acknowledge the opinions, values, and rights of other people.

Another word that has gained popular use is "absolutely." Like "definitely," "absolutely" is an unqualified word that leaves little wiggle room. If a contestant is certain that an unambiguous answer is what she wants, then that is perfectly acceptable. She must, however, be aware of the message that she is communicating.

One of my least favorite words is "hopefully." It is used constantly during pageants. "Hopefully" serves an opposite purpose from "definitely." Rather than being absolute, "hopefully" is a disclaimer. It is used by contestants to indicate a lack of firm conviction and to give the impression of sincerity and humility. "Hopefully, I can be a good titleholder" doesn't work.

Contestants often speak about their goals for the future. This is fine, if the question specifically asks about plans or expectations such as, "Where do you see yourself in 5 years?" However, many contestants describe scenarios that are based more on wishes and dreams. Too many of these kind of answers will lead the judges to question her credibility. During the interview, contestants need to concentrate on their accomplishments and what they have done, rather than what they will do.

Interview Tip: Whatever you say, don't say "whatever." It is an indication that a person has given up trying to communicate.

48. Balancing Polarities

Once you replace negative thoughts with positive ones,
you'll start having positive results.

– Willie Nelson, singer, songwriter,
activist (1933–)

I watched a national pageant in which the top five contestants were each asked different onstage questions concerning current events. The women were expected to deliver their answers in 30-second sound bites. First, it's difficult to say anything of substance in 30 seconds. Second, pageant contestants are notorious for giving generic, upbeat answers, which was the case in this pageant. Yes, everyone wants world peace, but no one seems to know how to achieve it. For the interview contestant, the challenge is to remain positive without disregarding the possible downside or complexity of an issue or question.

Each of us has a positive and negative pole, like a battery. Usually one of these polarities is dominant. Some people do nothing but complain, while others are intent on ignoring all of the bad things that happen. Given the choice, it is always best for the contestant to emphasize the positive. The negative pole repels, while the positive pole attracts people. Being negative requires a great deal of energy and gives little in return. However, a positive perspective is efficient and produces energy.

Remember, a pageant contestant is trying to secure a job, which will probably be won or lost during interview. A job seeker, who misrepresents herself, blames other people for her failings, or disparages fellow workers, is going to be shown the door. No one wants to hire a disgruntled worker. Thus, the interview contestant should concentrate on finding a way to respond positively to every question.

Of course, there are some questions that will have a negative connotation. These should be acknowledged. However, maintain an optimistic interview. Whenever negativity does enter the conversation, it can be minimized by turning toward the positive polarity.

A good example of polarity preference can be shown with the

common pageant question, "Why should we choose you as Miss _____?"
A negative orientation has the contestant comparing herself to the other
contestants. A more positive approach to the question involves affirming
the other contestants for their initiative in competing.

Interview Tip: Identify the positive and negative aspects of a
question by doing a force field analysis. Draw a line down the middle
of a piece of paper. On the left side, list all the positive components of
an answer as you can. On the right side, list the negative implications of
the answer. Then, give an answer that emphasizes the positive side while
acknowledging some of the negative aspects of the issue. Doing a force field
analysis will help you learn to think critically and to formulate answers that
are balanced and credible. Keep your answer concise and focused. You do
not have to include all data or ideas that you have.

49. The Supreme Court

Doubt yourself and you doubt everything you see. Judge
yourself and you see judges everywhere. But if you listen to
the sound of your own voice, you can rise above the doubt
and judgment. And you can see forever.

– *Nancy Lopez, professional golfer*
(1957–)

In the 2008–2009 season, All-American Renee Montgomery of the
UConn women's basketball team was considered to be the best point guard
in the country, leading her team to an undefeated season. However, during
the Big East Tournament, she only made 7 of 30 baskets and 4 of 9 3-point
shots. Did that stop her? Nope! Renee had 19 points in the first half of the
first National Tournament game. "I never think about things when I am
shooting the ball, except that it will be going in," she said.

Renee exemplified two important points. First, she did not dwell
on the past nor anticipate the future. She was in the present moment.
Secondly, Renee realized that every shot was not going to go in. Therefore,
she didn't allow a missed attempt to escalate into self-doubt. Every shot is
a new shot.

People judge themselves far more harshly than they judge others.
This is particularly true for women. It is unimaginable that our court system
would convict and sentence someone without evidence or a trial. Yet, we do
that to ourselves all of the time.

Suppose a contestant thinks she has given a poor answer. Because
she feels she has done badly, she loses her confidence and gives up on her
interview. However, what if the judges actually liked her answer and she
didn't realize it? If a contestant becomes the judge and the jury, she will
inevitably render the wrong verdict.

In a broader context, being less judgmental provides the time
and space to make accurate evaluations. Many judgments are conditioned
responses to situations and events. Others are the result of habitual
thought patterns. To become less judgmental, the first step is to become

a conscious observer of some of one's thoughts. It is like looking through a powerful telescope that reveals thoughts instead of stars. There is no need to see these stars as positive or negative. The simply exist in the vastness of space. Thoughts come and go. Unencumbered by the trial of self-judgment, the interview candidate will experience unprecedented freedom of speech.

Interview Tip: When you find yourself becoming judgmental, there is a quick way to extinguish that behavior. Mentally say, "Cancel." This known as a pattern interruption. It is like closing a computer file. The judgment program will shut down, enabling you to focus on the interview.

50. Trust the Process

There are no secrets to success. It is the result of preparation, hard work, and learning from failure.

– Colin Powell, four-star general,
Secretary of State (1937–)

The contestant was playing her flute. Suddenly, the flute flew from her hand and hit the stage with a loud thud. A collective gasp arose from the audience. She stood motionless for a moment. Gathering herself, she bent down, picked up her instrument, and resumed playing where she left off. Pageant judges admire a contestant, like this one, who responds to a mistake or accident with style and grace. There is no greater indication of character and poise.

One of the better pieces of advice I have given to many pageant contestants is that no one learns from winning. Like all absolute statements, there are notable exceptions. However, as a rule, winning and satisfaction are tantamount. When we fail to reach our goal, there is a tremendous opportunity to learn. No one gets better by being satisfied. In the moment, nothing takes the place of winning. In the long run, though, second, fourth, or even tenth place may be the best thing that ever happens. Learning to use apparent failure as a springboard to greater success is one of the secrets of champions. Losers are not people who don't win; they are people who give up.

Another obstacle that stands in the way of success is perfectionism. There is no such thing as a perfect world. Sometimes things are unfair, but most of the time they're not. Trying to control every word, movement, and perception is a waste of time.

I was once associated with a contestant whom the other competitors called "Helmet Head." Every hair was brushed and sprayed until it looked as though it had been glued in place. It was perfect, only it wasn't.

A contestant should allow herself to experience the unanticipated, spontaneous, memorable moments that give color and texture to life. The fact is that no matter how hard anyone tries, there are many things that are beyond one's control. Control what you can; let of go of what you can't. Trust the process.

Interview Tip: Research shows that what you touch can affect what you think. People who briefly held a cup of hot coffee judged other people to be more caring and generous than those people who held a cup of iced coffee. So, wrap your fingers around a warm beverage, and you will feel a greater sense of optimism about your interview.

51. Ways to Warm-up Interview Muscles

Games lubricate the body and the mind.

– Benjamin Franklin, U.S. founding
father, inventor, philosopher
(1706-1790)

Ashley called me just before her interview. Naturally, she was a little nervous. I assured her that she was well prepared. To prove it, I had her answer some of the questions that we expected she might be asked during the interview. As she became less self-conscious and more relaxed, her style and speech improved. Then, I sprang some unexpected questions on her. She paused, a little taken back, but quickly recovered her composure. She was warming up. Then, her answers to these unexpected questions became conversational and fluent.

By the way, she called me immediately after her interview. Her elation with her performance brought tears to my eyes.

Singers vocalize scales. Dancers stretch cold muscles. Athletes jog. Every competitor gets ready for his or her game or performance by warming up. Likewise, the pageant contestant needs to engage her interview "muscles." Most contestants go into the interview cold. But by doing a few exercises before the interview, a contestant will be able to perform at her peak level from the very beginning of her interview. The best way to warm up for an interview is to talk, talk, and talk. A contestant should visualize a successful interview, focusing on having a positive experience;

- talk aloud, either to someone or on the phone (if it is allowed);
- practice answering expected questions;
- relax by doing breathing and other exercises;
- distract herself from the interview by doing something else; and
- trust the process and herself.

Interview Tip: Once you have completed your warm-up exercises, you are done. Clear your mind by directing your attention to something else. Listen to music, read, or play a computer game. Do anything that absorbs your attention. Trust that your training and experience will take over. Remember, if you allow yourself to enjoy the experience, it will show.

52. Jelly Beans

Questions show the mind's range, and answers its subtlety.

– Joseph Joubert, essayist (1754–1824)

Pageant interview questions come in as many colors and flavors as a bag of jelly beans. Some are as common as cherry, while others are as exotic as dragon fruit. Questions can be as dense as dark chocolate or as sweet as cotton candy.

From favorite foods to the state of the national economy, a contestant can be asked just about anything. In general, pageant questions are less than challenging, which is unfortunate. Demanding questions allow a contestant to demonstrate her ability to think critically and to communicate effectively. A superficial question only means that the competitor must work harder to make her answer thoughtful and compelling.

Just as I recommended previously for contestants, I keep a collection of interview questions on my computer desktop. Whenever I think of an interesting question or come across a provocative topic, I add it to the list. To make things a little more manageable, my list is grouped by categories: general, interests, influences, goals, experiences.

Personal information. Family, pets, sports, hobbies, travel, and goals.

Fun. Music, art, drama, literature, television, movies, and popular culture.

Current events. Issues and events of local, national, and global significance.

Women's issues. Roles, relationships, rights, and responsibilities specific to females.

Metaphors. Comparisons that begin, "If you were a …"

Values clarification. Decision making based on conflicting choices.

Pageant. Motivation, goals, and experiences associated with pageants.

Platform. Issues and activities related to social concerns or community service.

Judges' favorites. Questions often asked of contestants.

Great questions. Archetypical, universal, multidimensional inquiries.

Interview Tip: Brainstorm questions by writing as many as you can, without regard to whether or not they will be asked. Then, divide them into categories. Make adding to this list a part of your pageant preparation.

53. Interview Prophecy

If you keep on saying things are going to be bad, you have a good chance of being a prophet.

– Isaac Bashevis Singer, author
(1902–1991)

From Egypt to Greece, the ancient world depended on prophets to predict the future. Whether by divine intervention (Biblical prophets) or an uncanny ability to calculate probabilities (Nostradamus), prophets had a strong social influence. Fortunately, one doesn't need a prophet to figure out some of the questions that the judges might ask.

Questions are usually specific to each contestant. They can be based on her platform, current events, values clarification, or simply what interests the judges. The possibilities are limitless. However, there are certain inquires that are common to all pageants.

Because the winner will be representing the pageant system, the judges need to know as much as possible about her, how well she communicates, and what kind of spokesperson she will be. Based on those broad areas of inquiry, the contestant can practice responding to probable questions. It should be understood that the purpose is not to prepare an automatic answer. Instead, the contestant should develop her thoughts and polish the way she expresses herself. A few examples of frequently asked questions are:

- What are your greatest strengths?
- What three words best describe you?
- Where do you see yourself in 10 years?
- What was the last book you read for pleasure?
- What sites would you show a visitor to our state?
- Who is your role model?
- How will you promote your platform?

Interview Tip: A good method for generating probable questions is to think about what you would ask if you were a judge.

DID I REALLY SAY THAT?

54. A Question of Bias

Women are always being tested...but ultimately, each of us has to define who we are individually and then do the very best job we can to grow into it.

– Hillary Rodham Clinton, first lady,
senator, U.S. Secretary of State (1947–)

Interview questions can be framed in three ways: pro, con, or neutral. Most pageant interview questions are pro—that is, their language and framing presupposes an optimistic response. For example, "What do you like about being a titleholder?" By its wording, the question assumes the contestant enjoys being a pageant queen. Conversely, "What don't you like about being a titleholder?" contains a negative bias. There is nothing wrong with this, since every endeavor has its share of rewards and challenges. The third kind of question is neutral, not slanted toward a positive or negative response: "How would you describe your experience as a titleholder?"

During September 2009, a controversial book was published that told the story of the murder of a family from the perspective of one of the alleged perpetrators. A heated controversy erupted in the Connecticut town where the crime was committed, over whether the town library should add the book to its collection. Members of the public were outraged that such a depraved individual could gain an audience and possibly sympathy, after what he was accused of doing. Community members also objected on the grounds that reading the book would be disrespectful to the husband/father who had survived. The library board took the position that denying shelf space for a book would be censorship.

In our state, it is customary for a local civic group to quiz the state titleholder. They asked Maggie if she thought the book in question should be allowed into the library. Can you detect the bias in the question? It is in the words, "be allowed." Inherent in this question was the supposition that purchasing this particular book required permission. Maggie was able to give a fair, credible answer to their question by being honest and explaining the complexity of the issue.

Everyone has an opinion. So, when a judge asks a question, he or she may well be predisposed to a certain point of view or ideology. However, regardless of the judge's bias, the contestant should remain true to herself. She should express what she genuinely thinks and feels.

Wherever possible, it is prudent to frame answers in a positive manner. Acknowledge any bias inherent in the question, but don't dwell on it. Rather than being negative or critical, a contestant should turn the question toward something affirmative that will support her answer.

Interview Tip: In your interview answers, take into account that there are multiple ways to answer the same question.

55. One Size Does Not Fit All

A major stimulant to creative thinking is focused questions.
There is something about a well-worded question that often
penetrates to the heart of the matter and triggers new and
ideas and insights.

– Brian Tracy, self-help author (1944–)

When in school, we take different types of tests. In elementary
school, we might have been asked to define a word. Then, in high school,
we had to finish a sentence with a word or phrase. During college, our
psychology professors gave multiple-choice tests, but history examinations
required long essays. Our art history electives tested our memory of names
and dates. Generally, there was a right and wrong way to answer all of the
questions, and we were graded on content rather than style.

Unlike objective tests, pageant questions are open-ended. There
are no correct answers. Presumably, if every contestant were asked the same
question, each answer would be different. The way that a contestant chooses
to respond is totally at her discretion. Whether someone loves Bach or the
Beatles, no one will try to tell this person who her favorite composer should
be. The challenge for a contestant is to make her answer so interesting that
the judges can hear the music.

There are two subcategories of open-ended questions: high gain
and low gain. High-gain questions require a certain level of knowledge
and analysis. They are substantive and can cover anything from politics
to women's roles. Any question that is sufficiently complex to require
critical thinking can be considered high gain. An example of a high-gain
question is "Do public figures, such as entertainers and athletes, have
an obligation to behave as role models?" A contestant's conclusion will
depend on whether she places greater value on personal or societal
responsibility. This is a complex issue for which there is no right answer.

Low-gain questions explore personality, taste, and cultural
preferences. They are subjective and are based on feelings more than
analytical ability. This does not mean that they are necessarily less

challenging than high-gain questions. Low-gain questions involve personality and experience rather than the consideration of ideas. Certain low-gain questions are open to broad interpretation. For example, "If you were a Disney character, who would you be?" Now, by itself this question is not exactly a brainteaser, but it affords the contestant an opportunity to be original and entertaining.

It is entirely possible to give a high-gain answer to a low-gain question. A simple question can have a profound answer. Low-gain questions also tend to provide a platform for the contestant to display her creativity, humor, and individuality.

Interview Tip: Practice answering both high-gain and low-gain questions. Make your thinking transparent by describing the process by which reached your conclusion. Express your personality by sharing anecdotes that are relevant to the question.

56. Show Your Smarts

Knowing a great deal is not the same as being smart. Intelligence is not information alone but also judgment, the manner in which information is collected and used.

– Carl Sagan, astronomer, astrophysicist, writer (1934–1996)

In the not-too-distant past, women were discouraged from pursuing classes in advanced math and science. Today, women are still paid less than men for the same work, and a glass ceiling exists that limits a woman's potential upward mobility in the corporate world. Regardless, women have excelled in every area and endeavor. Yet, there is still a subgroup of young women who choose not to fulfill their academic potential. They fear becoming isolated or having to take on nontraditional roles as the result of demonstrating superior intellect. These young women essentially sabotage their own futures.

An interview contestant should not be afraid to demonstrate her intelligence or to express her ideas. The days when a pretty face and long legs were enough ensure a pageant crown are fast disappearing.

No contestant should be reticent when it comes to showing that she is capable and well informed. As exceptional women like poet Maya Angelou, secretaries of State Condoleezza Rice and Hillary Rodham Clinton, and many others have demonstrated, a women's intelligence and personality are not mutually exclusive.

Intelligence is not confined to an IQ score. In fact, most of the people with astronomical IQs do no better in life than those with more conventional numbers. Howard Gardner, a professor of education at Harvard University, identified eight distinct types of intelligence. His theory of multiple intelligences explains something that everyone knows instinctively: there is book smart, and there is street smart.

I prepared Victoria for her state pageant interview over the course of several months. Although she had been a mediocre student and was unfamiliar with many issues, she was a quick study. However, her real gift was an innate ability to read people. She could charm the spots off a ladybug. Victoria had the knack for making each person feel as though he or she were the center of her attention. Dr. Gardner would say that Victoria had high interpersonal intelligence, which might otherwise be called people smarts.

A contestant does not need to have encyclopedic knowledge to appear intelligent. A well-spoken contestant who can communicate ideas and information will win the respect of the judges.

Interview Tip: You never know when some bit of obscure information will become useful during an interview. Gather facts, stories, and information from many sources.

57. Painting with Words

The greatest danger for most of us is not that our aim is too high and we miss it, but that it is too low and we make it.

– Michelangelo, painter, sculptor, architect (1475–1564)

Decades ago, scholars had concluded that Michelangelo was a painter insensitive to color. Then, in 1981, the Vatican announced its intention to restore the Sistine Chapel. It took 30,000 hours of work to restore the monumental artwork—twice as long as it took the artist to paint it. Centuries of water damage, humidity, and the residue of burning candles had covered Michelangelo's frescos with layers of grime. Beneath it, restorers found new, bright colors, as the artist intended them to be seen. Similarly, interview answers can be dull and lifeless. But if the contestant uses her words to paint a picture, her answers will be brilliant and bright, like the restoration of Michelangelo's frescos.

A contestant has the ability to paint pictures for the judges by employing descriptive language. Words can have color, contrast, tone, texture, and delicate shades of meaning. The interview contestant needs to use expressive language to create a visual sense. Consider two answers to the question: "What does spring mean to you?"

Answer #1. Spring is the transitional season that comes between winter and summer.

Answer #2. Spring is a sparkling dewdrop dripping from the red velvet bud of a new rose.

The first answer is scientifically correct, but it is detached and colorless. Answer #2 evokes an image that is tactile and symbolic. Which one do you think a judge is more likely to remember? Answers that involve multiple senses excite different parts of the brain, increasing their impact and satisfaction. During the interview, a contestant can invoke

- imagery to create a mental picture,
- adjectives and adverbs to elicit an emotional response,
- metaphors and similes to make direct and indirect comparisons,
- words that evoke a visual response,
- words that are associated with touch and feeling, and
- the right words to express nuance and the degree of meaning.

Interview Tip: Read poetry to learn how to use words descriptively.

58. The Gold Standard

As long as one keeps searching, the answers come.

– Joan Baez, folk singer, songwriter,
activist (1941–)

Serena had the potential to win. Her interview was the problem. Like most interview contestants, her answers were stereotypical. There was nothing particularly interesting or colorful about any of them. After her initial answer, she made oblique references to ideas that were already familiar to everyone. Plus, the more we practiced, the more she became intimidated by the whole process.

One evening, I told Serena to forget abstract ideas and to talk about herself. It was as if she became another person. Her face and body language literally changed. Fear disappeared. Serena was clearly excited and spoke confidently about her experiences.

The judges don't want an in-depth analysis of world politics or the causes of hunger in the Third World. They can read reports in newspapers and magazines. The judges want to know about the contestant; who she is, what she thinks, how she feels, and what makes her tick. The goal of every contestant is to communicate as much information about herself as possible. The great thing is that no one is better equipped to do this; you are the foremost expert on yourself!

Answers require more than sound bites but must be succinct enough to allow enough time for the judges to ask several questions. Besides the obvious qualities of intelligence and personality, the judges want to know whether a contestant can communicate effectively and how well she is able to perform under pressure. Thus, pageant interview answers need to be articulate, affable, and, most of all, entertaining. That is a daunting challenge. Understanding how to compose a quality answer is the first step in having a successful pageant interview.

Over many years, I perfected a method for teaching contestants how to give a quality interview answer. I call it the confluent method. By learning to answer in an interconnected sequence, a contestant has a framework for responding to almost any question. The heart of the confluent method is the contestant's personal story. By its nature, the personal story is original and entertaining. Answering in this way removes a contestant's fear, because all of the information a contestant needs is readily available. The interview becomes an experience to enjoy rather than to dread. The outcome of this method is a contestant who is confident, congenial, and excited about participating in the interview process.

Interview Tip: Learning to give confluent responses should be the long-term goal of every dedicated interview contestant. Like reaching the highest level in any activity, it requires knowledge, judgment, and lots of practice. Facility with language, a variety of personal experiences, and composure during the interview are prerequisites. Everyone can learn to give confluent responses. The first step is to understand the difference between a typical pageant interview answer and this proactive system.

59. The Default Response

No question is so difficult to answer as that to which
the answer is obvious.

– George Bernard Shaw, playwright
(1856–1950)

Over my years of judging and coaching pageant interviews, I have listened to contestants answer similar questions in very different ways. These have ranged from a single word to answers that contained in-depth analysis, psychological insight, and philosophical reflection. How a contestant chooses to respond depends on the nature of the question and how adept she is able at using the question as a platform to share information.

The "default response" gives a direct answer to a question, with little more. It is "bare bones;" there are no amenities or extras. Pertinent information and elaboration are minimal. The default response contains no complex ideas, vivid imagery, or personal narrative. Because it is reactive rather than proactive, it is strictly confined to answering the question. The default response is common among untrained, inexperienced contestants who assume that a simple answer is adequate.

There are questions to which default responses are appropriate. For instance, Kate was asked, "What would you do if your boyfriend hit you?" The timing, tone, and matter-of-fact answer that Kate delivered said as much as her words: "I would call the police." No further explanation was required. There was no room for negotiation or exceptions. Her resolve on this issue was abundantly clear. The power of her answer was vested in its directness and conviction. However, this is the exception rather than the rule.

Below is an example of a default response to a low-gain question.

Question. What is your favorite food?

Default response. My favorite food is macaroni and cheese.

There is nothing particularly original or exciting about the answer. It is no more interesting than the question. Default responses tend to be nebulous and lacking in details. They make the judges' job a burden.

Interview Tip: The default response is rarely the best response, although there are questions to which a brief response is appropriate. With practice, the contestant will develop the judgment necessary to make that decision. Meanwhile, learning to expand on an answer with personal experiences, concrete examples, and vivid description is the best course.

60. The Reflective Response

Every clarification breeds new questions.

– Arthur Bloch (1948–)

The reflective response is similar to—as they say in ads—a car that comes "nicely equipped." It is more than basic transportation, but not what we might call a luxury automobile. The reflective response provides more information than the default response, but is still little more than a reflection of the question. As I will later outline, there is still another level of response.

Most experienced interview contestants answer with some form of the reflective response. It usually begins by the contestant repeating the question and then giving her answer. That is followed by examples, ideas, or description. If a question asks for a personal opinion or evaluation, the contestant most often shares abstract ideas that she has heard or read. Typically, these concepts are simply restatements of others' ideas. The reflective response is the level that most contestants and managers consider optimal. However, it causes most contestants sound similar because their answers are reactive. They respond directly to the question and do not expand their answers to include additional information.

Question. What is your favorite food?

Reflective response. My favorite food is pizza. Whenever I go out with my friends, we order a pizza. It's my comfort food. I like my pizza with pepperoni and lots of cheese. My favorite place to have pizza is a small shop in the north part of town.

Here, the contestant first repeats the essence of the question. If this is done repeatedly, the contestant begins to sound like a parrot, though. Then, the contestant shares some personal information about favorites and where she likes to eat. The idea of eating with friends indicates a gregarious personality. Little details like that have a subliminal effect on the judges.

The contestant could have expanded her answer by talking about different styles of pizza. She could have discussed pizza toppings and her own experiences making pizza. There is an opportunity to talk about why comfort foods make us feel good. Ancillary topics such as families eating together could also be introduced. The obesity epidemic and the importance of physical fitness are spin-offs of this, as well.

Remember, interview answers are as flexible as a Slinky. They can be twisted and turned in any direction chosen by the contestant.

Interview Tip: One of our Junior Miss contestants answered a question about her favorite food with a rapid-fire description of at least a dozen ways to prepare chicken. By the time she got halfway, her enthusiasm and excitement had all of us laughing out loud. She conveyed an authentic sense of her personality without the least bit of self-consciousness. Low-gain questions often present the opportunity to show who you are more than what you think.

61. The Confluent Method

It is not enough to have a good mind; the main thing
is to use it well.

– René Descartes, mathematician,
philosopher, scientist (1596–1650)

The confluent response is like a luxury automobile. It has all
the options and a great deal of style. The word confluent means flowing
together, like a river that is fed by multiple sources. As stated previously,
the foundation of the confluent response is the contestant's personal story.
Because each person's story is different, confluent responses are unique
and memorable. A personal story can never be wrong. The confluent
response also neutralizes the fear of not knowing how to answer.

One of its great features is that it can be used to redirect a
question. The contestant can also comment on questions that may
not be asked. By doing this, she can interject information that might,
otherwise, never be communicated. Confluent responses will thus
influence subsequent questions that the judges ask. It is very much
like interviewing oneself!

Question. What is your favorite food?

Confluent response. There are so many foods that I really like, it's
difficult to choose. What immediately comes to mind is a dessert I had
at an Italian restaurant. Following a superb meal, I ordered the "chocolate
planet." It sounded just too good to pass up. When the waiter brought it,
I couldn't believe my eyes. There were three scoops of gelato—vanilla,
chocolate, and almond—drizzled with a handmade dark chocolate. That
would have been enough, because I love anything chocolate. But the
dish was orbited by what looked like a latticework of woven sugar. I still
don't know how they did it. Well, the whole presentation was celestial.
It tasted just as good as it looked. Yes, I think that is my all-time favorite
dish. As you know my platform concerns physical fitness. Intelligent

eating is certainly a big part of it. But once in a while, I think everyone deserves to indulge in something special. Then, it's back to eating smart!

This is a classic confluent response. The contestant responds to the question, shares a personal story, elaborates on the answer, and redirects the interview. It begins by acknowledging many choices, which indicates openness. She uses her choice of food to show her facility with words, creativity, and interpersonal skills. The description evokes vivid imagery. Describing the sugar as "celestial" is creative, and the childlike enthusiasm is contagious.

This confluent response allows the contestant to include details and information that the judges should know about her. The answer is personal, one-of-a-kind, and therefore striking. The conclusion confirms the answer and then redirects the question into another area. The apparent conflict between the platform and decadent dessert is reconciled, ending the answer on a positive note.

Interview Tip: Breaking away from reflective responses can be daunting. With practice, confluent responses will seem to flow as smoothly as steam.

62. The Anatomy of an Answer

Be willing to trust your instincts, especially if you cannot find answers elsewhere.

– Brian Koslow, author, entrepreneur

The confluent method uses a contestant's personal story as a prologue to her answer. This is called the narrative. The answer, which is illustrated in the narrative, is given in the interpretation. The elaboration provides an opportunity to expand and enrich the answer. Finally, the answer is reinforced and concluded in the summary. Together, these four sequential steps flow together to form a comprehensive answer.

The confluent response is, by far, the most effective way to answer a question. It is personal, entertaining, and informative. Learning the confluent method requires practice and dedication, though. It is a way of thinking and a process for communicating.

Narrative. The confluent method uses a story to introduce the answer. It is like a preface to a book. Having listened to the question, the contestant begins her answer by sharing a personal story, anecdote, or experience that is related to the question. The judges are far more interested in a contestant's story than an abstract answer that is bland and impersonal.

Interpretation. It is surprising how many contestants fail to answer the question. Sometimes contestants just get lost in their verbiage or simply forget the question. Other times, they are so tentative; they just circle the question, without giving a definitive answer. During the interpretation, the contestant extrapolates the answer from the narrative. The point of her story is the answer to the question.

Elaboration. Answering a question without supportive evidence is like convicting someone accused of a crime without a trial. After sharing a personal story and interpreting the answer, the elaboration allows the contestant to present evidence, ideas, data, or more examples to reinforce her answer.

Summary. Every well-written story has a beginning, middle, and end. The summary is the final step in the confluent method. By summarizing her answer, the contestant reiterates her position and indicates that her answer is complete. The summary puts an exclamation point on an answer.

Interview Tip: Contestants usually limit their interview preparation to mock interviews, but there are additional ways to hone speaking skills. Toastmasters and similar organizations provide opportunities for practice and critical feedback. Accept any opportunity to grant an interview or make a speech. Offer to be a master of ceremonies for an event or to introduce a speaker. Attend a town meeting, and make a presentation about an issue. Experience is a great teacher.

63. Telling Your Story

We all live in suspense, from day to day, from hour to hour;
in other words, we are the hero of our own story.

– Mary McCarthy, author, critic,
activist (1912–1989)

In 1998, CBS premiered an unusual television program. Host Steve Hartman used a dart to randomly select a town somewhere in America. Having done that, he began making phone calls until someone from that town agreed to be his subject. As many as 44 people, in one location, rejected his invitation. However, others were anxious to participate. Since then, Everybody Has a Story has received numerous broadcast and journalism awards. The program is a slice of real Americana, as told by ordinary people who have extraordinary stories.

If there is a secret to the pageant interview, it is that every contestant's goal should be to tell the judges her story. Note that I have not said that the goal is answering questions. Of course, a contestant must answer the judges' questions. However, she should view the questions as instruments that she can use to share her story. Here is an answer I use to demonstrate a good way to respond to a question.

Question. What is your favorite song?

Confluent response. My preference in music seems to change from day to day. I love Sinatra, female jazz singers, and oldies. On my way here, I was listening to one of my oldies CDs. A song by Ray Peterson, from 1962, has stuck in my mind. It's called "The Wonder of You." You might know it because Elvis had a big hit with this song. Actually, Elvis called Ray Peterson to ask his permission to record it. The lines in the song, "When no one else can understand me/When everything I do is wrong/You give me love and consolation/You give me hope to carry on . . . I guess I'll never know the reason why/You love me as you do/That's the wonder/The wonder of you." Isn't that a beautiful thought? I like the idea that we really

125

don't know as much as we think. So, "The Wonder of You" will always be among my favorite songs.

This is a textbook confluent response. It illustrates how a succinct response can be packed with information. Rather than ruminating over who actually is my favorite singer, I grabbed the first thing that came to my mind and developed it as I spoke. My narrative gave me time to make a decision and begin processing information. I happen to know something anecdotal about the song (that is, the writer and Elvis's relationship to it), so I added that to the mix. I then used the elaboration phase to explain what about the song appealed to me. In my summary, I concluded by reiterating my choice.

Interview Tip: Make a list of everything unique about you: family, pets, collections, life experiences, etc. Ideas will come to you as you think about it. Keep this list in your mental file.

64. Grab a Life Jacket, but Don't Abandon Ship

It's impossible now to walk past anyone and not realize that every single person is unique and has something worthy to say.

– Steve Hartman, broadcast
journalist (1963–)

When Tina didn't know how to answer—which was often—she froze like a deer in headlights. Sometimes, she would even cradle her head in her hands.

Everyone who has ever been interviewed has experienced that moment when she has absolutely no idea what to say. Panic! However, the confluent method is designed to be a life preserver. Using a personal story as a starting point, the contestant never has the sense of being dropped in the middle of a vast ocean. What derails so many contestants is the mistaken idea that every answer has to be correct. Before the question is out of the judge's mouth, contestants are scrolling through their memories, searching for the ideal answer.

Let's be clear—an interview is not a math test. There are no right answers. What makes a quality answer is a narrative that supports and explains the contestant's thinking. Again, more than anything else, an answer should reveal something about the contestant's personal story.

Question. Should the drinking age be lowered?

Default response. I don't think the drinking age should be lowered. It is fine where it is.

Reflective response. Yes, I think the drinking age should be lowered. If you are old enough to be in the military, you should be able to drink. Eighteen-year-olds are old enough to make their own decisions.

Confluent response. A few weeks ago, I was at a party. A small group of teenagers got together and chugged beer and whiskey until one of them threw up and another guy passed out. We had to drive them home. So, the incidence of binge drinking on college campuses and the number of drinking and driving accidents tells me that lowering the drinking age could be disastrous. Some teenagers are simply too immature to make good decisions. In essence, they need to be protected from themselves. In my opinion, the drinking age should not be lowered.

The default response is indicative of immature thinking. It lacks anything to support the conclusion. The reflective response is supported by an often-cited defense. The confluent response begins with a narrative that provides first-hand experience. Because it is a personal story, it is unassailable and memorable. The answer also indicates an awareness of the greater issue by referring to binge drinking and auto accidents. The summary takes a strong position, but tempers it by saying "some" not "all" teenagers are too immature.

Interview Tip: Instead of frantically searching for an answer, let your mind empty for a moment. It will fill with a thought you can use for your answer.

65. The Geometry of an Answer

A style is not a matter of camera angles or fancy
footwork, it's an expression, an accurate expression
of your particular opinion.

– Karel Reisz, filmmaker (1926–2002)

It's easy to tell the work of an amateur photographer. All of the pictures are taken from the same angle, which is usually directly in front of the subject. After viewing a few of these photographs, they all begin to look alike.

A seasoned photographer chooses angles that portray the subject in ways that viewers don't ordinarily see. I used to challenge my photography students to show me a familiar subject in a new way.

Answering interview questions is like taking expert photos. If the contestant habitually gives responses that are predictable, she will be overlooked. Instead, calculate new angles. Find an individual, unique, and creative way to answer a question.

Question. If you could have dinner with one famous person from history, who would it be?

Default response. I would have dinner with Jesus.

Reflective response. If I could have dinner with one person from history, it would be Joan of Arc. Her story has inspired me since I was a little girl. Joan of Arc was the first feminist, because she did things no other woman had done. I admire her willingness to die for her faith. I would like to meet Joan of Arc.

Confluent response. History is filled with characters that are larger than life. I actually have a fantasy in which I show Benjamin Franklin all of our modern technology. Imagine how astonished he would be by the automobile and Google? I would love to ask Thomas Jefferson how it felt to sign the Constitution. I would like to shake hands with Abraham Lincoln. I want to know if God really spoke to Moses. I would like to sit quietly with the Buddha, without saying a word. But most of all, I wish I could spend time telling my father what I have accomplished in the last 20 years. It would make him happy.

The default response is devoid of any elaboration or insight. The reflective response contains some interesting observations. Yet overall, the answer has the same problem as the amateur photograph; it doesn't shed any new light on the subject. Yet the confluent response separates itself by taking an oblique angle. Once again, the confluent response provides space to explore possibilities before leading to a conclusion. While the most contestants respond directly to the question, the confluent response reinterprets the question to make it more inclusive. It delivers far more information than the other responses. The contestant does not allow the narrow framework of the question keep her from expanding on the answer. The conclusion is like an O'Henry surprise ending. It provides still another unexpected angle.

Interview Tip: Unexpected angles make answers interesting.

66. Show and Tell

Tell me and I'll forget; show me and I may remember;
involve me and I'll understand.

– Chinese Proverb

Remember show and tell from elementary school? Everyone would bring something from home and tell the class all about it. When I was in third grade, I played my plastic, silver saxophone for my class. It was a big hit.

It is always better to show than to tell. This can be accomplished by employing specific examples, descriptive details, and words that have emotional content. Although I taught a course in advertising, I am still seduced by a good advertisement. Anything that is new or improved or promises to make me look younger in 10 days finds its way into my shopping cart. I know better, but still I succumb, because words have power.

Most interview contestants make the mistake of telling, rather than showing. Being descriptive is not just about using adjectives. Words come to life when they are anchored in descriptive details.

Question. What makes you happy?

Default response. My dog makes me happy. She is a miniature French poodle.

Reflective response. What make me happy? Shopping makes me happy. When I am upset, I go shopping. Buying something new always make me feel good.

Confluent response. I keep a small, framed piece of artwork next to my computer. It's a picture of a little boy holding a star on the end of a string, as if it were a kite. Written on the frame, in gold lettering, it says, "Dreams are almost always taller than you are—that way you have to reach to make them come true." Reaching for the stars makes me happy. I once read an article that said having achievable goals is the key to happiness. Learning about people, having personal goals, and appreciating the little things make me happy. I entered this pageant because it gave me the opportunity to have a new experience and make friends with other women. Challenging myself makes me happy.

This is another ubiquitous pageant question. Since happiness is a subjective state, most competitors relate it to significant objects or persons, all of which are external to that contestant. A problem arises when the answer lacks elaboration, as in the default response. There is nothing remarkable about the reflective response. In fact, it seems to indicate a rather shallow personality. The confluent response, however, takes a very unusual approach to the question by equating happiness with attitude. Although this answer is not about a picture, it is rich with detail that describes the picture, gold lettering, quotation, etc. The contestant validates her answer with a reference to an article. By relating this question to her motivation for entering the pageant, she anticipates a question that the judges might ask. Her summary is also clear and indicates her answer is complete.

Interview Tip: Try to involve the judges in your answers by using visual and emotional cues.

67. The Welcome Guest Knows When to Leave

Houseguests should be regarded as perishable: leave
them out too long and they go bad.

– Erma Bombeck, humorist (1927–1996)

Nancy had the gift of gab. She would go into a store and by the time she left, the clerk was her friend. She would talk with anyone about anything. Nancy seemed to be a natural for pageant competition. When the time came for her interview, Nancy was a practitioner of the philosophy, "If a little is good, more must be better." Her responses were way too long, thus becoming . . . boring.

Have you ever been a houseguest? The first few days are fun and exciting. But, after a while, what was novel becomes a burden. Answering interview questions is like being a houseguest. Stay too long and even the most hospitable host will wish you would leave.

Finding the optimal length for an interview answer is a puzzle that every contestant must learn to solve. There is no right length for an interview answer. Its duration will depend on the nature of the question, what the contestant wants to say, and how she says it. During the interview is not the time to worry about the length of an answer. By pageant time, the contestant should have practiced enough to have a feeling for the proper length of her answers.

There are two important rules that pertain to duration. First, stay on topic. Second, tie everything to the answer.

Many people take side trips when they give an answer. The problem comes when they lose their direction and end up somewhere they had no intention of going. Every part of an answer should have something to do with its subject. Another frequent contributor to overly long answers is rambling. Saying the same thing over, in different words, makes the answer travel in never-ending circles. Most times, less is more.

Sometimes the connection between a part of the answer and the subject is not immediately apparent. The contestant has to be careful to establish a relationship among all parts of the answer. Learning to see and make relationships is called "pattern recognition." It is a form of creative thinking and will raise the quality of any interview answer. Don't assume that the judges will recognize all of the relationships. So, a contestant must be careful to show them explicitly how her ideas relate to one another.

The confluent method is designed for show and tell. A contestant should use the narration to illustrate her answer, the way an artist uses a brush. In the summary, she should connect all those strokes to her focal point by showing how they are related. The result is a unified composition that makes a beautiful picture.

Interview Tip: You don't have to say everything. Learn to be selective. Include ideas and experiences that will only animate your answer.

68. Every Orchestra Needs a Conductor

Conductors must give unmistakable and suggestive signals
to the orchestra—not choreography to the audience.

– George Szell, conductor, composer
(1897–1970)

My interview on a television program devoted to books and
authors was scheduled a year and a half in advance. One would think that
would have been enough time for the host to prepare. From the moment
he began, though, it was obvious to me that he hadn't read my poetry book.
Instead of being annoyed, I took the opportunity to direct the conversation
toward the topics that I wanted to discuss. In essence, I became my own
interviewer.

Most pageant interviews are like a tennis match; the judge serves a
question, and the contestant returns an answer. The flow of information is
severely limited. Yet answers can be expanded to include information that
was not directly requested by the judges.

The contestant can use most interview questions the way that
a scientist utilizes a catalyst to cause a chemical reaction. The simplest way
to do this is by going beyond the answer. Rather than merely answering the
question, the contestant can add things that she wants the judges to know.

There is also the domino effect in interviewing. One category leads
to another. This is a form of creative thinking. If a contestant is asked about
her platform, she could add something about a book that is related. An
answer about a film or literary character can become a discussion of role
models, celebrities, pop psychology, art as imitation of life, or how to change
the oil in a car.

Information inserted at the end of an answer can lead the judges
to the next question. This creates a seamless transition into the next
question. By offering some intriguing bit of information, the contestant
invites further inquiry. For example, if asked about sports, a contestant
could add the fact that there is a controversy as to whether cheerleading
is a competitive sport, deserving Title IX (that is, equity of treatment and

opportunity in athletics for women) recognition. This could lead to follow-up questions about her opinion of whether cheerleading should be considered a sport, her participation in cheerleading (if applicable), Title IX and women in business, or the way different cultures treat women.

Contestants do not have to wait for a question that may never be asked. Being proactive allows the contestant to guide the judges.

Interview Tip: Don't wait for the question that never comes. Whether or not they specifically ask, create opportunities to tell the judges what you want them to know.

69. Making Questions Disappear

To me, being "politically incorrect" means the opposite
of being political—which means to spin everything.
That's all it's ever meant to me. It's never meant
liberal or conservative. It means honest.

– *Bill Maher, comedian, host,
social critic (1956–)*

When something negative is reported, most people try to put a positive spin on it. For instance, there are many instances of pageant winners being caught doing everything from misrepresenting personal information to abusing drugs. Tears are shed, apologies are issued, and a negative behavior is reshaped into a character-building event.

Public relations experts, who know how to put a positive twist on negative events, are called "spin doctors." The interview contestant can learn something from them. One of their favorite techniques is called "deflection." This is the practice of redirecting an answer into an area in which the person is better versed or more comfortable. This should not be confused with "stonewalling," in which a direct answer is purposely avoided.

Contestants can use deflection when they don't know an answer but want to respond anyway. Deflection carries inherent dangers. Diverting a question may fail to answer it or be interpreted as stalling. However, successful diversion is so seamless that no one is aware that it is happening.

In a study at Harvard Business School by Todd Rogers and Michael I. Norton, people watched or listened to small parts of political debates. The speakers were rated on how well they were trusted and liked. The politicians who strayed far from the topic were rated poorly. But, talking about similar issues did not bring the same result. Subtle changes in topic often resulted in the listeners forgetting the question. In fact, people preferred the speakers who digressed slightly over those who were more direct but incorporated a lot of verbal hitches into their speech.

The interview candidate, who speaks with authority and ease and expands the subject, can avoid being knocked off balance by an unfamiliar question. Carrying the conversation into something tangential to the question is a skill that every interview contestant should practice.

Interview Tip: Deflecting an answer is like driving a car. You can steer your answer in any direction, as long as you stay on the road.

70. African Trade Routes and Other Answers

To be a person is to have a story to tell.

– Isak Dinesen (Baroness Karen von Blixen-Finecke), author (1885–1962)

Kara and I were discussing plans for her next mock interview. She said that she preferred our one-on-one practice sessions. Indeed, it was during one of these sessions that she seemed to "get it;" she called it her "interview epiphany." I was trying to explain to her that it was possible to talk about anything, by extrapolating a few pertinent facts.

As I explained to Kara, many contestants give up if they are not totally sure about a subject, but that shouldn't happen. For instance, if I were asked about African trade routes—something I know nothing about— during an interview, I would say something like this:

> Honestly, I don't know anything about African trade routes, but I do know something about factors that influence trade. In Third World countries, there are three factors that typically influence trade: climate, infrastructure, and safe passage. Issues like rainfall, the availability of transportation and the quality of roads, and, of course, freedom from raiders all influence the ability of a country to bring indigenous goods to the market. With hostile climates, undeveloped transportation systems, and law-lessness, trade in rural areas of Africa can be difficult, though far from impossible.

There is nothing in this answer that an 8th grade social studies student doesn't know. Yet it sounds erudite and convincing. Although I have no idea what made me chose African trade routes as a subject, this particular demonstration resonated with Kara. Modeling answers was valuable way for her to learn how to interview.

As previously stated, mock interviews are an important part of preparation. Even nominees to the Supreme Court hold mock interviews prior to their confirmation hearings. A coach who knows a contestant well can accomplish a great deal during a private session; thus, I am a firm believer in personalized instruction. One of my personalized training methods is Question of the Day (see Chapter III). A few months before the pageant, I begin e-mailing my contestants one question each day. They reply, and I critique their answers for content and word use. Writing an answer to a question is not the same as verbally responding to a question that one has never heard—it's a bit like training for the Tour de France on a stationary bicycle. However, it helps contestants learn to think critically and to clarify their ideas. It also is a great way to make them gather information about every subject under the sun. I also use the Question of the Day to make contestants prepare for the questions that are typically asked. Finally, it also helps contestants learn what to include in an answer.

A question is like a seed in the core of an apple. Each one has the potential to yield exquisite fruit. Granted, some questions are easier to answer than others. However, no question is too difficult or too trivial that it cannot be answered in an extraordinary way. Words are important, but so are the myriad of other factors that contribute to a great answer.

Interview Tip: Go beyond the answer.

71. Questions without Answers

I was gratified to be able to answer promptly. I said,
"I don't know."

– *Mark Twain, American author*
(1835-1910)

Everyone can't know everything. On rare occasions, a question asked during an interview is so obscure that no one can be expected to know the answer. If a contestant is guessing, it will be painfully obvious. In such cases, passing does no harm.

There is, however, a caveat. Ordinarily, pageant questions involve subjects that a well-informed contestant should be able to answer. Passing on a question that she is expected to answer will diminish her interview. Therefore, it is key that a contestant only pass on a question that is so specific or technical that there is no reasonable expectation of knowing an answer.

Mara called me one evening. Her voice betrayed concern. She had been ruminating about an answer she gave during her interview. "Did I say the right thing?" she asked. I reassured her that she had responded appropriately. Although it was a local pageant, the interview had been quite demanding. Later, she told me that her local interview had been far more demanding that her interview at the state pageant.

Perhaps because she was a pre-law major, one of the judges asked Mara, "Do you know which state mandates that a mother play Mozart to her unborn child?" No reasonable person could expect a contestant to know this obscure bit of trivia. Mara responded with appropriate deference: "No, I don't know, but I would appreciate it if you would share that with me." All of the judges smiled. Mara's response actually worked better than if she had known the answer. She showed the judges her intellectual curiosity and demonstrated respect for the judge who asked the question. Mara turned an awkward moment into a win–win situation.

How to answer when the contestant is unsure is a judgment call. Many times, I have noted that answers—and platforms—contained misinformation. The safest, most ethical course of action is to be candid. It is fine for a contestant to say that she is unsure of certain facts, figures, or details. As in life, honesty is the best policy.

Interview Tip: It is better to have nothing to say than to speak and say nothing.

72. Critical Thinking

We should be teaching students how to think. Instead,
we are teaching them what to think.

– Clement and Lochhead, 1980,
Cognitive Process Instruction

Years ago, when Sony announced its intention to pursue legal action against individuals who downloaded songs illegally, I thought there might be a teachable moment in this. I asked my students, "Do you think it is acceptable to download songs to avoid paying royalties to the artist?" A lengthy discussion ensued. The overwhelming consensus was that it was perfectly reasonable, because, as Sophia put it, "Everyone does it, so it's all right." No amount of discussion or debate could convince Sophia to reconsider her position.

Sophia's bandwagon ("everyone is doing it") approach to thinking is flawed. The goal of the interview contestant is to convince the judges that she is capable of analyzing an issue, evaluating information, and drawing a rational conclusion—which demonstrates critical thinking.

Pageant contestants have become notorious for superficial and sometimes convoluted answers. They offer opinions when analysis is appropriate or analysis unsubstantiated by the facts. Either way, such answers are inadequate. Granted, the length of a pageant interview allows little more than a sound bite. Interview questions usually are focused on opinions, rather than a body of knowledge. However, this in no way eliminates the need for critical thinking.

Nothing is more impressive to the judges than explaining the process by which a contestant arrives at her opinion. Consider the question of downloading music. This is a complex issue, involving the law, property rights, ethics, and cultural practices. If a song is an artistic property, owned by the musician who created it, is that person entitled to monetary compensation each time someone plays the recording? On the other hand, if a song is art, can anyone truly own it? Ultimately, these questions may have to be answered in court. However, the fact that the

143

practice of sharing downloads is ubiquitous doesn't simply make it right.

Interview Tip: A good way to practice critical thinking is to debate two different viewpoints on one issue for 60 seconds. First take one side, and then argue for the other. Be sure to support your conclusion by making reference to facts, examples, and anecdotes.

73. Transparent Thinking

Thinking isn't agreeing or disagreeing. That's voting.

– Robert Frost, poet (1874–1963)

Interview coaches are notorious for telling contestants what to say. Such answers are easy to identify; they sound scripted and superficial. Doing this makes a mockery of the interview process, and such contestants are bound to fail.

Every contestant needs to understand that everyone thinks in different ways about different issues. Critical thinking is only one way to solve a problem. Creative thinking produces new ideas that might not have been possible through traditional logic. Sir Arthur Conan Doyle's iconic creation, Sherlock Holmes, was the embodiment of deductive reasoning.

Just as someone can learn to play the piano or hit a baseball, different methods of thinking can be taught. Some ways we think include the following.

Logical thinking. Uses chains of reasoning to reach a conclusion.

Deductive thinking. Extrapolates from a single thing to many things.

Inductive thinking. Extrapolates from many things to a single thing.

Lateral thinking. Produces original ideas by solving problems in new ways.

Scientific thinking. Draws conclusions from empirical observation.

Intuitive thinking. Provides insight, based on previous experience and knowledge.

Comparing and contrasting. Examines similarities and differences.

Cause and effect. The relationship that causes one thing to effect another.

Interview Tip: Learn to think about the way you think, and you will you be able to understand how and why you make decisions.

74. Ambivalent Answers

I happen to feel that the degree of a person's intelligence is directly reflected by the number of conflicting attitudes she can bring to bear on the same topic.

– Lisa Alther, author (1944–)

Interview contestants have often said to me, "I don't know what to think." As I have stated in a number of ways, what to think is what you think. Opinions are opinions precisely because they are subjective. Who we are, how we think, our experiences, family backgrounds, values, and even our taste influence our opinions. What gives an opinion validity is the way it responds to the known facts. Still, two persons, who have the same facts, can reach entirely different conclusions.

So, what does a contestant do if she is ambivalent? If a contestant is asked a question about which she has information, but not a definitive opinion, transparent thinking—which is integral to a confluent response—is a viable alternative. By actually talking out both sides of an issue, she can compare and contrast information. In the process, she gathers enough insight to reach a conclusion. Or, her conclusion can be that she is unable to reach a conclusion. Most of the time, showing flexibility is better than being dogmatic.

Question. Do Barbie dolls send the wrong message to little girls?

Confluent response. I took a graduate course in art history, which required that we visit galleries in New York. On one of our visits, we saw an exhibit of Barbie photographs. The doll was placed in poses that ranged from mundane to provocative. Our instructor spent more than an hour discussing the symbolic meaning behind the art. Later in the day, we returned to the gallery, in a driving rainstorm, to hear the artist speak. She was a grandmother, from Long Island, who had simply taken the pictures of her granddaughter's doll. Then, not long ago, I heard of a woman from England had over 100 operations to try to look like Barbie. Now, that's beyond reason. Many authorities claim that Barbie dolls have a negative influence on young girls because no woman can emulate her proportions. And, what we experience when we are young often paves the way for what we become. Women come in all shapes and sizes. It's important for all women to learn to accept and honor themselves as they are. As far as Barbie dolls contributing to negative self-images, I don't know. Perhaps we need some more research in this area. But, to paraphrase Sigmund Freud, sometimes a doll is just a doll. I am not sure if Barbie is good or bad for kids, but a lot of girls have wonderful memories of her.

In this instance, the answer is a combination of information, experience, and speculation. There is no definitive conclusion. The inference of the introductory story is that you can read too much into anything. The story about the British woman is an interesting anecdote. Personalizing the information by describing experience adds credibility. The contestant does take a strong position against stereotyping. She demonstrates a deal of common sense and humility in her exploration of the issue.

Interview Tip: Ambivalence is not the same as indecision. Learn to recognize the difference.

THE ART AND SCIENCE OF INTERVIEW

75. A Question of Values

Values are not just words; values are what we live by.
They're about the causes that we champion and the
people we fight for.

– *John Kerry, senator, war hero (1943–)*

Values are the beliefs, principles, morals, and standards that guide a person's behavior. They can be religious, cultural, social, political, or aesthetic. Most societies have shared value systems that revolve around laws, behavioral norms, and even manners. For example, in America, it is considered rude for someone to cut in a line to get to a better position.

Contestants can expect to be asked questions that explore their values. These can range from questions about making ethical decisions to those that present conflicting alternatives. "If $10,000 was mistakenly deposited into your bank account and no one would know, would you keep the money?" This question explores a contestant's moral and ethical values. Other kinds of values questions present choices that reveal personal priorities. "If you could be one or the other, would you rather be rich or famous?" This question limits the answer to two similarly attractive alternatives. Having to choose one or the other creates ambivalence. The internal conflict is the essence of values-based questions.

The often asked, "Are you in favor of the death penalty?" is another example of a values-based question. There are many pieces of relevant information that must be taken into account to make an informed decision—the nature of the crime; mitigating circumstances, like childhood abuse; intelligence; intent; criminal history; social justice; and the chances of mistaken conviction. Yet, the decision to be in favor of or against the death penalty is most likely to be determined by the personal values of the contestant. Such factors as religion, reverence for life, and societal responsibility play pivotal roles. There is no right or wrong answer. The most effective way that a contestant can answer a values-based question is to demonstrate and explain the process of

149

her decision making. In doing so, she reveals her personal value system, which should be strong, thoughtful, and clear as a titleholder.

Interview Tip Practice answering a series of values-based questions as a way of clarifying your personal beliefs.

76. When Values Conflict

Human beings are perhaps never more frightening
than when they are convinced beyond any doubt that
they are right.

– Sir Laurens van der Post, author
(1906–1996)

The five finalists stood, waiting to draw the number of the celebrity judge who would ask her onstage question. The questions were contemporary and controversial, which was a change from the fluff of most past pageants. "Should the government bail out financially failing institutions?" "Do you think there should be a national health care system?"

Miss California, Carrie Prejean, was asked if she supported states legalizing gay marriage. Her response triggered a firestorm of controversy. She said:

> Well, I think it's great that Americans are able to choose one or the other. We live in a land [where] you can choose same-sex marriage or opposite [sex] marriage. And you know what? In my country, in my family, I think that I believe that a marriage should be between a man and a woman. No offense to anybody out there, but that's how I was raised and that's how I think that it should be—between a man and a woman.

It was evident to everyone watching that the judge who asked the question did not like her answer.

Miss California became the first runner-up to the Miss USA title that year. She told the news media that she believed her answer had cost her the crown. The judge who asked the question said that she should have answered not as Carrie, but as Miss USA. The state director also stated that Miss California should have answered the question with more compassion. This dramatic episode demonstrates the difficulty in answering values-based questions. Personal values are deeply ingrained, emotionally charged, and are often based on religious convictions. Topics such as abortion, homosexuality, religion, and politics are values-based. It is unlikely a contestant can give an answer that will be endorsed by every judge. However, as the saying goes, it is not what you say, but how you say it.

Some interview coaches advise contestants to tone down their opinions by taking a neutral position on any controversial issue. However, I advise contestants to tell the truth as they see it. The key to answering a values-based question is the understanding that everyone's point of view deserves to be acknowledged and shown respect. In my experience, a contestant who honestly presents her opinion will be appreciated more than someone who tries to please everyone.

Miss California could have framed her answer in a more inclusive and deferential way. The deciding factor is the contestant's ability to make it clear that her answer represents a personal value, rather than a declaration for the way everyone should live their lives. In my opinion, Miss California's attempt to be inclusive came across as superficial and disingenuous. Differing values do not have to be conflicting values.

Whether a more appropriately framed answer would have changed the outcome, I cannot say. Sometimes, taking a position exacts a toll.

Interview Tip: If you respect the right of other people to hold values that may be different from yours, you will be able to express your own values without appearing dogmatic or rigid.

77. Landing the Job

Be who you are and say what you feel, because those who
mind don't matter and those who matter don't mind.

– Dr. Seuss (Theodor Seuss Geisel),
author (1904–1991)

Before Tony Award-winning actress/singer Kristin Chenoweth
starred on Broadway and TV, she competed in pageants. In her
autobiography, Ms. Chenoweth wrote that she entered pageants so she
could perform on national TV and attract a theatrical agent. As young
women enter pageants for all kinds of reasons, it is important for a
contestant to understand and be able to articulate why she chose
to compete.

When I begin coaching a contestant, in fact, that's the first
question that I ask. Unfortunately, the usual response is, "I don't know."
Some women enter pageants with grandiose expectations, believing
that winning a title will transform their lives into a fairy tale. Like Ms.
Chenoweth, others hope that their talents will launch a career. It is good to
have goals. It is wise to have perspective. It is best to compete for the sheer
joy of the experience.

Facing the judges is like interviewing for a job. Having previously
submitted her résumé, she has to convince them that she is the right person
for the job. To accomplish this, the contestant needs to demonstrate how
her skills are applicable to the job requirements, what contribution she
can make to the workplace, and what distinguishes her from the other
candidates. She must directly or by inference answer the question,
"Why should we choose you for this job?" To give a credible answer, the
contestant has to reflect on her reasons for entering the pageant.

The rules for a pageant interview are the same as those for any
other job. A contestant should
- illustrate her comments with examples,
- show how her skills relate to the job,
- avoid comparing herself to others,

• never speak negatively about another contestant,
• be proactive in discussing her strengths, and
• know three reasons why she will be a good titleholder.

Interview Tip: Thinking of the pageant as a job will help you identify skills and attitudes that set you apart from the other contestants.

78. Standing on Your Platform

The most exhausting thing in life is being insincere.

– Anne Morrow Lindbergh, aviator,
author (1906–2001)

Awhile back, I created a program called Neighbors Helping Neighbors. It involved high school students and teachers doing volunteer work for elderly and disabled town residents. We cleaned, raked leaves, made small repairs, and even painted houses. We had been doing this for a number of years, prior to volunteer work becoming a high school graduation requirement in Connecticut. The idea was that by doing volunteer work, kids would find out how rewarding it can be.

Although I am a strong advocate of volunteerism, I opposed the idea of making it mandatory to graduate high school. Requiring students to perform community service makes it a job, and that changes the experience, in my view.

Quite similarly, many contestants adopt a cause for the sole purpose of using for it their platform. Since it does get the contestant involved in community service, it is always a good thing. However, judges can usually spot when someone is less than dedicated to their cause. One certain giveaway is the time frame of the volunteerism.

To make a platform more than a temporary affiliation, the contestant has to demonstrate a sincere commitment. This involves having a history with the organization, knowledge, experience, and passion. It is mandatory that the contestant is able to describe a platform's goals, activities, and outcomes. Most importantly, the contestant has to demonstrate her motivation and role in the organization. It's likely, although not definite, that a contestant will be asked about her platform during the interview. One of the most important goals of the contestant is to convince the judges that she is sincerely dedicated to her platform cause.

Most platforms—with negligible differences—have been used by other competitors in other pageants. It is not uncommon for two women, in the same pageant, to have the same platform. Therefore, each contestant has to present her cause in a way that makes it appear unique.

Almost any personal, community, or social cause can be the basis for a platform. Petra's platform promoted the therapeutic uses of music. She had spent years performing for elderly and disabled patients, so her platform was a natural extension of what she was already doing. Petra did a great deal of research, interviewed music therapists, and studied the mind–body connection. As a result, she was able to identify how specific types of music affected physiology. About a year after she won her title, Petra was invited to present the keynote speech at a conference. After discussing her platform, Petra actually proved how music can alter blood pressure, in a demonstration that involved the entire audience. Her talk was a hit.

Interview Tip: A contestant's description of her platform should be inspirational enough to make the judges want to join her program.

79. Advertising You

Advertising is fundamentally persuasion, and persuasion
happens to be not a science, but an art.

– William Bernbach, advertising
creative director (1911–1982)

While I was shopping at the local bed and bath store, a display caught my attention. "As Seen on TV," the sign read. This alone was enough to pique my interest. Like everyone else, I am susceptible to the persuasive power of infomercials. What would I do without my Snuggie? The trinkets were marvelous things: hangers that promised to end the clutter in my closest, fat-fighting grills, machines that killed bacteria with steam—all kinds of things that I didn't need.

Advertising is the art and psychology of persuasion. To convince the consumer to buy a particular product, the advertiser claims—or more accurately, implies—benefits. Most products have what is known as parity, that is, they are about the same. Let's face it: any laundry liquid will get clothes clean. What separates one product from another is not how they perform, but how they are perceived. Perception is the result of delivering a strong message combined with powerful visuals.

Advertisers know that emotions prevail over reason. That's why candy and magazines are placed near the cash register. People grab them on impulse as they are waiting to check out. Another psychological technique used in advertising is association. Words like "American," "mother," and "freedom" are associated with certain values and experiences. Ads use music, images, and words that are carefully calculated to make people feel good. This feeling is transferred to the product by association. The sight of a baby playing inside a tire delivers an entire message without speaking a word. The persuasive ad has emotional impact, creates an image of safety, and is memorable.

The interview contestant can use some of the same techniques that advertisers employ to sell a product. Be bold. Answers that are tentative or apologetic are not believable. A contestant should display the confidence that comes from the conviction that her product is worthwhile. Begin with the package. Advertisers know that bright colors draw attention to the product. A contestant should wear clothing or accessories that introduce color and energy to her appearance. A bright silk scarf or an artistic pair of earrings are expressions of individual taste and can provide a topic for conversation.

Then, emotional impact comes as the result of answers that are original and personal. As previously discussed, answers that tell a story create associations that remain well beyond the interview. I still remember judging an opera singer who told us about how she could put a sandworm on a fishhook. There was a certain incongruity between this lovely young woman and the nasty worm that made her seem like a regular person, someone to whom the judges could relate. Answers that have the judges nodding their heads in agreement, smiling, and sliding forward to hear more are eliciting an emotional response.

Like an advertisement, contestant image is a combination of appearance, impact, association, and perception.

Interview Tip: As part of your preparation, you should practice delivering a 30-second "Commercial of Self" in front of a mirror. Try to incorporate what you have learned about product advertising into your personal message.

80. Branding

A brand for a company is like a reputation for a person.
You earn reputation by trying to do hard things well.

– Jeff Bezos, CEO (1964–)

I have a pair of ultra-light, ultra-expensive Nike running shoes. The iconic Nike swoosh makes them instantly recognizable. When I wear these shoes, I feel like I could run in the Boston Marathon, only I really can't.

The Nike image has been carefully crafted to make people feel young, healthy, athletic, and most importantly, cool. This branding, coupled with a quality product, has made Nike a household name that is recognized even by non-athletes. People trust brand names. In consumer tests, people will buy brand name items, even if generic versions are substantively equal and less expensive. Branding is a powerful motivational force.

In advertising terminology, the pageant contestant is the product. The judges are the target audience. To impact this demographic, the contestant needs a marketing plan. She has to create an image—a brand—that will differentiate her from the other products. Her image should be derived from her unique personal story.

Some pageant systems actually require each contestant to submit a written marketing plan. Once again, in these, contestants tend to say similar things. They promise to be role models, make appearances, promote the pageant, and leave a legacy of love.

Research suggests that the brain responds to narratives that have a specific structure. Thus, a contestant's brand should be unique, vivid, and memorable. It should be emotionally engaging and rich in visual imagery. Remember, branding becomes memorable when it makes an emotional connection.

Here are some guidelines for a contestant:

Packaging. Become memorable by wearing something personally symbolic.

Performance. Show how her accomplishments relate to

what she will do as titleholder.

Credibility. Demonstrate that her plan is achievable.

Emotional appeal. Share her humor, humility, and moral compass.

Connect. Interest the judges with her personal story.

Imagery. Use metaphors and vivid descriptions to draw a visual picture.

Identity. Establish her brand as unique and distinct.

Interview Tip: Convince the judges that you are a product that they cannot do without.

81. Did I Really Say That?

Laugh at yourself first, before anyone else can.

– Elsa Maxwell, socialite, author
(1883–1963)

During the 2007 Miss Teen USA Pageant, Miss Teen South Carolina was asked, "Recent polls have shown that one-fifth of Americans can't locate the United States on a world map. Why do you think this is?" Her answer was so incoherent that she became the poster child for dumb pageant answers. Millions of people tuned into YouTube to see her performance.

To her credit, she appeared on The Today Show, where she showed that she could give a lucid answer to the question. Asked how she felt onstage, she replied that she drew a blank, misunderstood the question, and made a mistake. At one time or another, all of us do or say something we regret. Fortunately, it is not on national television.

Miss Teen South Carolina actually described what can happen during an interview rather well. A contestant can say everything well, but one slipup and it all can come undone. However, a contestant cannot be intimidated by the fear of making a mistake. If she does make a gaffe, she is in prestigious company.

On August 11, 1984, President Ronald Reagan, unaware that the microphone was on, joked, "My fellow Americans, I am pleased to tell you today that I've signed legislation that will outlaw Russia forever. We begin bombing in minutes." The lesson to be learned from this is that the microphone is always on. Treat everything you say as if it were being broadcast.

Even the articulate President Barak Obama is not immune from misstatements. Appearing on The Tonight Show with Jay Leno, he compared his lack of bowling prowess to that of a Special Olympian. Whoops! The President did not mean to disparage anyone. He is strong advocate for people with special needs. He was, in fact, being self-deprecating. Remember, any statement that remotely appears to disparage another person or organization should never be made.

Former President George W. Bush was infamous for his verbal blunders. At a rally in Florence, South Carolina, he said, "Rarely is the question asked, "Is our children learning?" Remember the discussion about the importance of using correct grammar?

If a contestant makes a mistake, she must deal with it on the spot. For example, President Obama immediately called the director of the Special Olympics and apologized for his unintended slight. Don't dwell on errors. Acknowledging and correcting a gaffe can actually elevate a contestant.

Interview Tip: Laughter is a balm that can soothe any wound.

82. The 45-Second Interview

When your work speaks for itself, don't interrupt.

– Henry J. Kaiser, industrialist
(1882–1967)

From the first word, the content of every book, every play, and every drama is aimed toward a conclusion. The ending can follow a sequence of events to a predictable result or come as a complete surprise. Character development, plot, conflict, suspense, and action are brought to a climax in the finale. Sometimes, the ending is happy and satisfying; others are tragic.

The need to sum up what has come before and to draw a conclusion is not confined to literature, however. Pageant contestants are usually given the opportunity to present a formal or informal conclusion to their interviews. These 45 seconds should be the most memorable moments of the interview.

The pageant interview summary can be approached in a number of ways. The goal is always the same: the contestant must make the judges feel that she is the best choice for the title.

The conclusion is a condensed version of the interview, with a few additions. The contestant should use the confluent method by integrating her story into the summary. Her summation should answer the following questions:

- What accomplishments, skills, or experiences do I bring to the title?
- Why do I want to be Miss _____?
- What is distinctive about me?
- How will I carry out my duties?
- What do I want you to know about me that you haven't asked?

Although this may seem like a lot of information to share in 45 seconds, it is eminently feasible. Like a politician who prepares talking points, the contestant needs to plan ahead of time. Not only will having a plan make the summary fluent, it will relieve some of the tension associated with performing under a time constraint. This is not to say that everywordneedstobepremeditatedandrehearsed.Planningasummaryislike having an outline or notes. It is a guideline, not a script.

Finally, this is the time to tell the judges anything that she wants them to know that wasn't shared during the interview. Everybody loves a happy ending. The contestant should be sure to end the summary on a positive note, such as how much she has enjoyed the interview, being part of the pageant, or meeting the other contestants. She should take advantage of the summary to make herself memorable.

Interview Tip: The summary should not feel like you are running a sprint. Maintain a pace that is urgent, but not rushed.

83. Onstage

When you stand on the stage, you must have a sense that
you are addressing the whole world, and that what you say
is so important the whole world must listen.

– Stella Adler, actress and acting
teacher (1901–1992)

Karin elected to take my photography class when she was in high school. She was a superb student. After she graduated from college, I encouraged her to enter a local pageant. She prepared well and enjoyed the process. Her platform was at-risk children. As is often the case, the judges chose their on stage question from the contestant's platform. She was asked, "How is a child identified as being 'at risk'?" Karin hesitated. She and I had prepared for everything except that question. Her answer probably cost her the crown.

Being onstage is different from the private interview. Standing alone and in front of a large audience can be intimidating. The amount of time allotted for the answer is extremely brief. In fact, the answer is usually more of a sound bite than a measured response. Many contestants appear defensive, rather than proactive. Answers usually come across like dramatic readings.

However, the onstage answer does have many things in common with the private interview. It should have a narrative and elaboration. To the extent possible, it should be conversational. Despite the pressure, the answer should not be rushed. It is important to give an unequivocal, assertive answer. Rather than giving a predictable response, the contestant should show her confidence and poise by being expressive and animated.

Laugh out loud. She should not deny her anxiety. It is natural to be nervous. So, she could think of something funny. Laughter stimulates the pleasure centers of the brain. Then, she will walk onstage with a smile.

Practice positive self-talk. Under pressure, it is easy to imagine everything that can go wrong. So, a contestant should practice positive self-talk. The truth is that she is prepared and has practiced precisely for this moment. The judges are on her side. The onstage question will be about something familiar to her.

Make a point. Nine out of ten times, onstage answers are a direct response to the question—without any elaboration. However, the onstage answer does not have to be minimal. The contestant should include a personal example that illustrates her answer. Also, she should be sure to highlight all of the important points that support her conclusion.

Slow down. Most contestants rush through their answer. To some extent, this is the fault of pageant directors, who warn contestants to make their onstage answers as brief as possible. Yet no one is going to take a hook and yank someone from the stage. The onstage answer is like Cliff Notes to a book. Even so, she should take as much time as she needs to deliver a complete answer.

Interview Tip: Before you answer your onstage question, take two breaths. This will help you process the question and give the impression of a contemplative person.

84. Knock on Wood

The best way to sound like you know what you are talking about is to know what you are talking about.

– Anonymous

Using a podium is an option in many pageant interviews. Podiums have been associated with public speaking since the days of the ancient Greek orators. Sermons are delivered every Sunday from church pulpits. Traditionally, the pulpit is used to rest a speaker's notes. President Obama reads from a teleprompter but still delivers stirring addresses from the dais. Since the pageant contestant has no notes, using a podium is purely a matter of personal preference. In other words, she should stand where she feels the most comfortable.

The podium will not disguise poor communication skills nor inadequate answers. Contestants who think they can hide behind a podium are making a big mistake.

Using a podium does have several advantages. It can feel like a life preserver in a big ocean. The podium grounds the contestant by giving her something solid to touch. Using a podium automatically establishes interpersonal distance and provides a point of departure and return for each answer. If the contestant does not know what to do with her hands, she can rest them on the dais.

Tanya asked me if she should use the podium for her state interview. I recommended that she stand to one side of it. Tanya has the long, lean figure of a model. In fact, she is a model. I wanted the judges to experience the full impact of her height and striking good looks.

Standing beside the podium removes some of the formality from the interview. Having a barrier between a contestant and the judges can inhibit a contestant from being expressive with her arms and hands. When the contestant is parallel to the podium, she is closer to the judges. This makes the interview seem more intimate. While she can stand on either side of the podium, I usually advise a contestant to go to the far side of the podium. This gives the judges more time to watch the contestant walk.

Being further from the door will make the contestant appear more at ease in the room.

If a contestant prefers to use a podium, there are a few things to keep in mind. Speakers tend to use the podium for support. Do not lean on the podium. Maintain good posture. The hands can rest lightly on the surface of the podium. Avoid holding the sides of the podium in a death grip. Some contestants drum their fingernails on the podium. The judges will find this to be really annoying. Thus, it is a good idea to practice standing at the podium until it seems natural.

Interview Tip: Try answering questions while standing next to and behind the podium. Become comfortable in both positions.

85. Interview Etiquette

Good manners have much to do with the emotions. To make them ring true, one must feel them, not merely exhibit them.

– Amy Vanderbilt, etiquette expert
(1908–1974)

It has always seemed to me that good manners are simply about being considerate of other people, not antiquated rules. Nevertheless, surveys indicate that common courtesy has declined over the last several decades. Because they didn't know any better, I have seen many contestants breach pageant protocol. A contestant doesn't have to know which fork is for the escargot, but there are certain standards of pageant etiquette. She should

- limit her introduction to a greeting and her name;
- never refer to the judges by their first names;
- not interview the judges;
- only shake hands with the judges if it is appropriate;
- not fidget, tap her fingernails, play with her hair, nor twist her jewelry;
- stand behind or parallel to the podium;
- never make wisecracks or clever remarks;
- leave jokes to comedians;
- not speak negatively about other contestants; and
- thank the judges at the conclusion of the interview.

Interview Tip: Respect, courtesy, and consideration will never be wrong.

DID I REALLY SAY THAT?

86. What to Wear

Fashion can be bought. Style one must possess.

*– Edna Woolman Chase, fashion
editor (1877–1957)*

After the woman I coached became fourth runner-up, I tried to obtain feedback from the judges about the areas that needed improvement. Most of the judges were forthcoming and offered constructive criticism. Quite by accident, I happened to overhear one judge talking about my contestant. He was highly critical of the color of her pantyhose. To this day, I wonder if he detracted points for something so trivial.

The clothing a contestant wears during her interview is important not only because of the way it makes her look, but also because of the way it makes her feel. If she feels attractive and well dressed, her overall confidence will be enhanced. The interview outfit is an expression of the contestant's personality, taste, and style.

Whether to wear a suit or dress may depend on the pageant directors. For many years, the business suit was the standard. With some pageants attempting to change their image, dresses have returned. Regardless, the contestant should select her outfit with care. Although there is no shortage of dress-for-success advice books, there is no formula for what looks best on a contestant.

A contestant should begin by deciding if she wants to wear a business suit or dress. She also has the option of mixing and matching a skirt or pants with a top. Then, she must select the color, fabric, and style that suits her. If the colors are so bright that the judges need sunglasses, or the suit is more appropriate for a funeral than a pageant, it is too extreme. Feelings are a reliable guide to matching colors, but a second opinion is always a good idea. Avoid busy prints and patterned hose.

Accessories give an outfit personality. Try to find one item—scarf, necklace, earrings, etc.—that has a history. It may be an antique pearl necklace that belonged to a grandmother or a turquoise ring from a trip to New Mexico. Not only will this be fashionable, it will provide a personal

171

story that could be told during the interview. There is a certain sense of security that comes from wearing something familiar and cherished.

Finally, a contestant must be careful with perfume. If a cloud of fragrance announces her presence before she enters the room, she has overdone it.

Appearance does not depend on a single garment. A contestant's visual impact is a combination of many elements. She should strive for a look that is unified and harmonious. The interview outfit should be in concert with the contestant's energy, emotions, preferences, and personality.

Interview Tip: The outfit should never divert attention from the contestant.

87. Food for Thought

Fatigue makes cowards of us all.

– Vince Lombardi, football coach
(1913–1970)

Pageant contestants do not always have the best eating habits. In a misguided attempt to maintain their figures, some contestants literally starve themselves before and during the pageant. Not only do they lose the muscle mass that gives a woman pleasant curves, they fail to provide their bodies the fuel to compete at an optimum level. Remember, the pageant is more like a marathon than a sprint. Sustaining energy and focus throughout interview, talent, evening gown, swimsuit, and onstage question requires quality nutrition and a reasonable eating plan.

I am not a physician, nutritionist, dietician, nor a particularly good chef. I do like to eat, though. My experience using food to enhance performance comes from research, athletics, and pageant coaching. I certainly do not intend to tell anyone what she should or should not eat. I am not an advocate of fad diets; rather, I believe in the value of a balanced diet. Certain foods will help contestants be alert, energized, and focused, while others will have the opposite effect.

Foods can also calm and support performance. For example, people who consume 1,000 milligrams of vitamin C before giving a speech have lower levels of cortisol and lower blood pressure than those who are deficient in the vitamin. Sugar and fat can inhibit cognition, deplete energy, and make one crave more. Further, high doses of sugar will provide an initial jolt of energy. The body reacts by increasing the production of insulin. The initial jolt of energy that comes from the sugar will be inevitably followed by an energy crash.

Here are some foods that will help a contestant perform her best:

Breakfast. Complex carbohydrates promote the production of serotonin and jumpstart the brain.

Protein. Eat a low-fat source of protein, like low-fat cheese, lean meat, or plain yogurt.

Whole grains. Carbohydrates that contain fiber are absorbed more slowly.

Coffee. Can improve cognition and mental alertness.

Water. Dehydration saps energy.

Nuts. A source of good fats and calming vitamin E, zinc, and B vitamins.

Oranges. These provide vitamin C and potassium.

Yogurt. Low-fat, plain yogurt is a good source of calcium, which has a calming effect.

Berries. These are delicious and filled with antioxidants.

Dark chocolate. Eat a piece of dark chocolate; it activates the brain's pleasure center.

Interview Tip: Don't change your eating habits close to a pageant. In fact, eating properly should be part of a contestant's pageant preparation.

88. A Touch of Humility

The moment of victory is much too short to live
for that and nothing else.

– Martina Navratilova, tennis
champion (1956–)

The same ritual is repeated at the end of every pageant. A newly anointed winner tearfully accepts her crown and an armful of flowers. She acknowledges the judges with clasped hands, as if offering a prayer. The tiara is hastily pinned on her head, at a rakish angle. She waves to the applauding audience and mouths the words, "Thank you, Mom!" However, being a winner is about more than a moment. For the next year, she will be representing herself and the pageant system.

As soon as the crown is placed on her head, the winner becomes a public figure. This means that people and the pageant system will expect a high standard of behavior. If she says something inappropriate, someone will be listening.

During a local pageant, one winner was overheard—by a pageant official—saying something to another contestant that could be called "bathroom humor." The official made it a point to tell everyone who would listen exactly what she had said. A Miss Teen title-holder held a party at her house while her parents were away. Allegedly, alcohol was served to underage teens. She was arrested and suspended from performing any activities associated with her title. Her indiscretion was the lead story on the nightly news. Vanessa Williams was forced to vacate her title of Miss America after revealing photographs, taken years before, surfaced.

The titleholder who behaves irresponsibly will be remembered. The queen who performs her duties with dignity and class will be respected. To remain grounded requires a well-defined sense of self, a strong support system, and a large dose of humility. It is too easy to believe one's press clippings. Does a public figure have a moral obligation to act as a role model? Think about it.

As a postscript, be careful what you put on YouTube, Facebook, and similar social networking sites.

Interview Tip: When you compete in a pageant, you become a public figure. People will be watching how you behave and what you say. All your good work can be undone in a moment of indiscretion.

89. Trust Yourself

We must be willing to let go of the life we have planned,
so as to accept the life that is waiting for us.

– Joseph Campbell, writer, lecturer
(1904–1987)

The mayor called me. I had begun coaching him just before he was elected. He wanted to discuss his last speech. "I could have made my points better," he said. However, he had received numerous compliments about what he said.

Sometimes, people's preconceived notions of how something should be prevent them from appreciating how good they are. I could always tell when the mayor was overthinking what he wanted to say—his speech would become halting and strained. Conversely, when he spoke, as he put it, "from the heart," he was much more fluent.

Remember what it was like to learn how to type? We had to think about where to place each finger, and there were lots of typos. Eventually, we all learned to type without giving it a second thought. Pageant preparation is like that; when the mock interviews are done and hundreds of questions have been answered, it's time to let go.

Allowing instincts to take over during an actual interview will make a contestant spontaneous and natural. The contestant who trusts herself will appear comfortable and enthusiastic. She will welcome unanticipated questions as opportunities to show her ability and be creative.

Interview Tip: Don't take yourself too seriously.

90. Graduation Day

Your chances of success in any undertaking can always
be measured by your belief in yourself.

— *Robert Collier, motivational*
author, (1885–1950)

Her interview was scheduled for 3:20 pm. As the time approached, I became fidgety. By 5:00 pm, I was downright nervous. I lay in bed at 11:00 pm, unable to fall asleep. Then, the phone rang. I checked caller ID, relieved yet apprehensive. What would I hear? Her voice was told me everything. "I think I won the interview award." A flood of joy and relief overcame me. When you work long and hard, success is sweeter than a chocolate ice cream cone on a hot August afternoon.

I cannot stress enough that the contestant's state of mind is the most crucial aspect of interview readiness. This means feeling competent, confident, and excited about talking to the judges. The preparatory process should begin 3 nights before the interview. Just as she is falling asleep, the contestant should visualize her perfect interview in complete detail. She should suggest to herself that she will feel relaxed and ready for the interview. This self-hypnosis will have a beneficial effect on her state of mind and performance. Another good way to prepare is to recall how a really good interview feels. She should think of a mock interview or coaching session when she was in the zone. Remember, the best interviews happen when one loses herself in the conversation. Self-consciousness disappears, and words flow effortlessly.

During the hours before the interview, the contestant must find something fun to do. About 30 minutes before the interview, I like to personally warm up the contestants whom I coach. Alternately, I use a cell phone or e-mail, depending on the situation. If conversation is impossible, contestants can warm up by talking in front of a mirror. Below are a few warm-up questions that will engage a contestant's mind and promote positive feelings.

• If you had three wishes, what would they be?

- What is your idea of a great day?
- What makes you happy?
- What are you reading?
- If you were a character in a novel, who would you be?
- What is your greatest accomplishment?

Interview Tip: Warming up mobilizes your mind just as putting your car into drive prepares your car to move.

91. Interview Choreography

Some stories don't have a clear beginning, middle, and end. Life is about not knowing, having to change, taking the moment, and making the best of it, without knowing what is going to happen next.

– Gilda Radner, comedienne, actress
(1946–1989)

Miranda's interview introduction was choreographed as methodically as a dance. Knowing the importance of first impressions and how the beginning and ending of the interview are most likely to be remembered, we scripted her entrance. The first thing that the judges saw was a tall, attractive contestant whose graceful walk personified energy. She turned and faced the judges, smiled and waited for two beats before speaking.

We chose "Good afternoon" as her greeting. It is indicative of good manners without appearing contrived. However, it is generic. We wanted her entrance to stand apart from the rest, without appearing contrived or cute. Since Miranda was the final contestant, we knew the judges would be somewhat desensitized or fatigued. So, I advised her infuse her salutation with sunshine. "I am happy to be here again," followed her salutation. The key word is "again," which gives historical information and sets up more questions. This is exactly what it did. Her next phrase was, "I was in the pageant last year. It was such a good experience that I decided to come back." From these words, the judges received a picture of an optimistic, friendly, tenacious young woman, the kind of contestant whom they want to represent the title.

To paraphrase an old aphorism, luck favors the well-prepared contestant. We had anticipated many of the questions asked of Miranda. She responded to other questions spontaneously, showing confidence in her ability to handle anything she was asked. People standing outside the room could hear the judges' laughter. She charmed the judges and took advantage of every opportunity to share information about herself.

A story about a wayward politician happened to break just before her interview. The question, "Where do you get your news?" flowed into another question, "What is the latest news?" Because she had watched the midday news, Miranda was able to share a "juicy" tidbit that demonstrated she was accessible, in touch, and down to earth. It served to further strengthen her interpersonal relationship with the judges.

Her closing was also prepared in advance. Miranda said, "Thank you. I've enjoyed talking with you. Have a good day." Once again, the right words can make a huge difference.

Miranda enjoyed her interview, and the judges enjoyed her. She won the interview award.

Interview Tip: If you enjoy the interview, the judges will enjoy you.

92. Pageant Postscript

Don't hurry, don't worry. You're only here for a short visit.
So be sure to stop and smell the flowers.

– Walter C. Hagen, golfer (1892–1969)

The commentators were talking about women's professional golf. They commented that not winning is not the same as losing. Initially, I didn't understand. They went on to explain that finishing in the top 10 of a golf tournament requires a really good game, as it's very difficult to win at the professional level.

Many women enjoy their first pageant more than any other precisely because they have no expectation of winning. Free from the crushing pressure of competition, they are able to enjoy the experience. If the contestant competes again and winning becomes more plausible, everything changes. Having invested time, energy, and money in preparation, leaving without a crown can be disappointing.

Yet like professional golfers, every contestant needs to realize that participating in a pageant is a remarkable accomplishment. She is among a group of select women who have the courage, physical gifts, talent, and support system to compete. Every contestant should be celebrating her achievement, never lamenting loss. In the course of a lifetime, the importance of the pageant will fade. I sent this e-mail to Cassandra:

> As you prepare for your interview, think of me as being in the room with you. In many ways, I will be. Close your eyes concentrate on your breathing, and recall the superb interviews you have given, last year and this year. Remember how you felt, how easy it was to talk, and how you were filled with energy. I am confident that your interview, this year, will be the best of them all.

The night before the final competition, I told Cassie that I couldn't finish writing this book until the competition was over. The pageant finals were held Saturday night. There were 10 semifinalists, then five. It came down to two women. Everyone held their breath.

Cassie won the state title, looking every bit the classic pageant queen.

    Interview Tip: Whether she wears the crown or not, every contestant is a winner.

93. Appreciate Yourself

We tend to forget that happiness doesn't come as a result
of getting something we don't have, but rather of recognizing
and appreciating what we do have.

– Frederick Keonig, inventor
(1774–1883)

Congratulations! Entering a pageant, let alone winning, is an accomplishment. A pageant contestant is doing what only a small number of women do. It takes motivation and courage to perform, answer questions, and face the judges. It also requires certain gifts. Someone who is too short, too stout, or sings like me is obviated from the competition. In his book, Outliers, Malcolm Gladwell makes the case that highly successful persons are not only the products of talent and hard work, but also the time period and circumstances that made their success possible. The same is true for pageant contestants. In reality, we do not do anything alone. The women who competed before and the people who supported a contestant are an integral part of the pageant.

People find all kinds of ways to make themselves unhappy. They dwell on what was, deny what is and worry about what will be. The book that taught me the power of poetry is Without, by Edward Hall. It is a heart-wrenching collection of poems chronicling his wife's—the poet Jane Kenyon—struggle with cancer. I heard him read from the book on a hot, Sunday night in August. I was sitting at my computer, listening to his interview on the local public radio station. The words and emotion within them transfixed me. I was frozen in the moment. I felt my throat closing and my eyes watered. I realized how fragile life can be and how fortunate we are to be exactly where we are.

Whenever you feel the tendency to be critical, dismissive or negative about yourself, just think about all the wonderful gifts you have been given. Be grateful, for there are so many who have so much less.

The pageant is a unique event. It does not measure accuracy, strength, or endurance. The winner doesn't run the fastest race or capture all of an opponent's pieces. Pageants are about perception. Winning depends on another person's judgment of a contestant's performance and personality. Many contestants get caught up in making comparisons to competitors. Thinking that another contestant is more talented, articulate, or attractive sows seeds of self-doubt. Everyone has moments of insecurity. At those times, being grateful can balance the scales.

Appreciate the opportunity you have been given, your relationships, and your accomplishments, one of which is being in the pageant. The more familiar a person becomes with something, the greater the tendency to take it for granted. Even if you do not get what you want, be grateful for what you have.

Interview Tip: Try your best, and you will never have regrets.

III. A DOZEN DAILY QUESTIONS

Be master of the mind rather than mastered by the mind.

– Zen Proverb

The Question of the Day is like a vitamin supplement. It aims to strengthen a contestant's knowledge and to contribute to the health of her interviews. To obtain its full benefit, the Question of the Day must be taken regularly. It takes time for this supplement to work, but the results are sure to be impressive.

I developed the Question of the Day as a coaching method for contestants who needed to expand their knowledge base and to learn how to construct answers. It requires contestants to choose relevant information and to compose a concise answer. It has proven to be highly successful.

The Question of the Day is also a distance learning technique that allows me to provide instruction conveniently via e-mail. About 2 months before a pageant, I begin sending similar questions to the contestant. The contestant then responds to my e-mail with her answer. I provide critical feedback and some words of encouragement.

Indeed, writing an answer is certainly not the same as standing in front of a group of judges. A contestant cannot use the cut, paste, or delete function in her actual interview. There will be little time to think over or to reconsider an answer. That said, as a method for developing critical thinking skills, the Question of the Day is a valuable addition to any contestant's interview preparation.

In this chapter, the responses to the Question of the Day are based on my personal responses or fictional responses. Because I am a man—an older man—the content of some of these answers is quite different from what a contestant would probably say. Regardless, they are intended to demonstrate the narrative quality of the confluent response.

Remember, the brain has an intrinsic attraction to stories. The best answer is always based on a personal story. To do this, a contestant needs to learn how to make associations. By connecting several disparate events or ideas, an original answer can be shaped. This is the essence of creative thinking. The ability to find relationships means that one will never be at a loss for an answer.

In the coach's commentary, I share an analysis of the response. First, there is a default response, which is little more than a one- or two-word answer. This is followed by a reflective response, which is how many contestants respond to questions. The reflective response is like a mirror that reflects an image—it often begins with the questions being repeated. It will become obvious that both of these answers lack narrative, elaboration, and evidence of critical thinking.

In contrast, the confluent response is rich in all the characteristics that make a compelling answer. A contestant should note the importance of words and their influence on perception in the examples provided. Also, she should understand how the narrative is tied to the conclusion.

Although some are more challenging than others, the questions in this chapter are representative of those that can be expected during a pageant interview. Remember, it is not the nature of the question but the quality of the answer that matters. Before reading the answers, I suggest that the contestant attempt to respond to each question herself. By taking her daily dose of questions, it is my hope that a contestant feels confident and energized during her actual interview.

Question of the Day #1

Don't be consistent, but be simply true.

– *Oliver Wendell Holmes, Jr.,*
Supreme Court justice (1841–1935)

Question. If there were an 11th Commandment, what would it say?

Default response. I don't know; probably I'd say don't text when you're driving.

Reflective response. If there were an 11th Commandment, I think it would say that everyone should try not to use cell phones or to text while driving. I have seen lots of people talking on their cell phones while they are driving. I think this is very dangerous.

Confluent response. If I recall correctly, there was another set of commandments, which Moses threw to the ground when he came down from Mount Sinai and saw the Israelites partying. So, there actually was an 11th Commandment. But if I had my way, the 11th Commandment would say, "Thou Shall Not Text nor Talk on the Cell Phone while Driving." This is one of my pet peeves. I have seen distracted drivers chatting on their phones, texting, or even reading their iPads. They drift to and from lanes, and go too fast or too slow. A New England Journal of Medicine study, in 1997, found that the risk of collision was four times greater when the driver was using a cell phone. Harvard researchers estimated in 2002 that one in 20 traffic accidents involved drivers talking on a cell phone. I find it very interesting that researchers compare driving while phoning or texting to drunk driving. In my state, talking on a handheld cell phone is illegal, yet people simply ignore the law. Like Moses, it angers me to see people jeopardizing their future and the future of others. So, I would like to see my 11th Commandment become universal law rather than a suggestion.

Coach's commentary. This is a question that requires the contestant to be creative and spontaneous. It could have been answered in a million different ways. The default response is "bare bones," lacking any kind of elaboration. The reflective response adds a bit more context, but not enough. There is no narrative, references, or even data to make it interesting and convincing. The confluent response, however, is full of details, personal experience, and factual validation. This response begins with a reference to the Old Testament, showing familiarity with the Bible. Moses's smashing of the tablets is compared to the anger induced by distracted drivers, which reinforces the Biblical component. This response is built on a self-disclosed personal pet peeve, which is another question that is often asked during pageant interviews. This answer is also given credibility through statistical support. It is a very convincing argument, couched in a narrative and supported by data.

Contestants think they have to give a definitive answer to every question. During an interview, though, a contestant doesn't have time to think about everything she knows, feels, and has experienced. Most often, the first thing that pops into her mind is a good place to start. She might give an entirely different answer under other circumstances, but no one knows that—nor does it matter. It is not the answer as much as the narrative that she connects with it that will impress the judges.

So, a contestant should trust herself, make a decision about her answer, and make it come alive.

Question of the Day #2

When nothing is sure, everything is possible.

– Margret Drabble, author, biographer,
critic (1939–)

Question. What are three words that best describe you?

Default response. Happy, fun, and loyal.

Reflective response. I would have to say that I am loyal, honest, and fun to be around. My friends and family are very important to me, and I would do anything for them. I always tell the truth, and I love to have a good time. I recently went to an amusement park and had so much fun.

Confluent response. I have a close friend, with whom I have competed for 25 years. We ran road races against each other, rowed in indoor rowing championships, and still have a photography contest every season. I do all that I can to win because I love to compete. Competition brings out high performance. We are the fiercest rivals, but when he wins, I am happy for him. That is loyalty. We tell each other what we think without fear of hurt feelings or rejection, because we have respect for each other's opinions. That is honesty. The payoff comes when the loser of our contests has to buy the winner breakfast. Have you ever seen anyone eat eggs, pancakes, and French toast, all together? It makes me happy to watch my friend enjoy his victory meal so much—"to the victor belongs the spoils." That's being a good friend, even when I lose. So, I think it is fair to say that I am competitive, loyal, and honest.

Coach's commentary. The default response offers nothing to support the contestant's answer. The reflective response is impersonal and generic. It is notable for what it lacks, rather than what it contains; it is devoid of details and validation. Anyone can say anything. It is up to the contestant to confirm what she says by showing who she is by what she has done.

Responses that contain examples and stories are much more concrete. A narrative adds interest and color to this response. The confluent response covers a lot of ground in the very first statement.

Instead of speaking in generalities, I have cited my friend and followed that with a piece of information—25 years—that validates our friendship. There is an intriguing tension in this answer; we are close friends and rivals at the same time. This is demonstrated by our athletic competitions followed by our celebratory meals. The fact that we respect each other's opinion gives this answer greater depth and resonance. Note how each of the examples is tied to a specific quality associated with the friendship. An answer can never be too clear.

Finally, the list of breakfast foods brings a touch of lightness to an otherwise serious answer. The quotation shows that I don't take myself too seriously. The end of the answer reinforces the three qualities, just in case they have been forgotten or lost in the story.

Question of the Day #3

To the uneducated, an A is just three sticks.

– A. A. Milne, author (1882–1956)

Question. Are politicians, athletes, and celebrities obliged to behave as role models?

Default response. Yes, I think they should act as role models.

Reflective response. If you are a famous person, you should act appropriately at all times. A lot of people look up to famous people. Some of those pop singers who use drugs are setting a bad example for kids. I think Miss America is a good role model.

Confluent response. I am ambivalent about this question. It seems as though all you have to do is pick up a newspaper to read about some athlete who has used steroids, a pop singer who is on drugs, or a politician who has cheated on his or her spouse. Being famous doesn't make you responsible or bestow good judgment. These people are negative role models, especially for the young people who see them as idols. Celebrities make huge amounts of money from the very people for whom they seem to have such little regard. In this country, we have the freedom to make our own choices. It takes a well-developed sense of self to resist the temptations of too much money and unconditional adulation.

That's why I admire people like Maya Angelou and Jimmy Carter. I think that famous people by virtue of their constant visibility should behave in an exemplary way. On the other hand, being famous does not take away the right to behave badly. However, if someone breaks the law or the rules of the game, he or she should face the consequences.

I think people need to take a step back and realize that celebrities are ordinary people with extraordinary talents. People shouldn't confuse talent with character. In the end, how a person behaves is a choice, not an obligation.

Coach's commentary. This values-based question involves social norms, personal rights and obligations, responsibility, and freedom, among other issues. It is complex and requires an answer that shows introspection and acknowledgement of different perspectives. The credibility of the answer depends on how it is framed, supported, and demonstrated.

The default response shows no underlying thought, while the reflective response fails to acknowledge the complexity of the issue. It contains absolutely no evidence of introspection or insight. In addition, the concluding comment about Miss America being a good role model could be interpreted as self-serving. It sounds shallow and superfluous.

The confluent response begins with the admission of ambivalence. Good—it is not always necessary to take an unconditional position on a topic. Then, comparing and contrasting opposing views about the question displays critical thinking. The idea that celebrities have an obligation to fans is counterbalanced by the concept of individual freedom. The answer depends on how values are weighed. It soon becomes clear that this confluent response supports good behavior on the part of celebrities, but does not demand it. However, toward the end, the answer takes an unexpected turn, suggesting that the fans need to be less worshipful and more realistic when it comes to famous people. That is a creative response to the problem. Thus, the confluent response demonstrates how exploring both sides of an issue can result in a convincing answer.

Question of the Day #4

I think everybody should get rich and famous and do everything they ever dreamed of so they can see that it's not the answer.

– Jim Carrey, actor and comedian
(1962–)

Question. If you could possess only one of these coupled traits, would you choose to be: beautiful and wealthy, intelligent and charming, or athletic and famous?

Default response. Gosh, this is hard. I would choose to beautiful and wealthy.

Reflective response. I don't know which one to choose. They're all good. To be honest, I would probably choose to be beautiful and rich. Everyone would pay attention to me. I think it would be fun to be beautiful and rich. I would have a fabulous social life!

Confluent response. I feel like a little kid in a candy store. Should I choose the maple butter creams, the peanut brittle, or the dark chocolate bark? My mother used to take me to a candy shop that actually made all of those candies.

Being beautiful and wealthy would seem to be everything anyone could ever want. But, both beauty and money are transient. Physical beauty fades, and money does not ensure happiness. I would love to be athletic, because I enjoy sports and admire athleticism. Athletes can become famous and earn a lot of money. But that, too, fades. I think it is sad to have reached your peak by the time you are 25 years old. So, intelligence and charm are the qualities I would choose. Intelligence is a gateway to everything else. Charm is the rare ability to connect with other people. Intelligence can be used to make a contribution to humanity, and charm would allow me to exert a positive influence. Intelligence and charm are like chocolate truffles and jelly beans—an irresistible combination!

Coach's commentary. The default response shows nothing beyond its answer. The reflective response is more developed, but it implies a rather

195

self-involved individual. It may be an honest answer, but it is pretty shallow. Plus, I am always suspect of people who say, "To be honest…" Does this mean that they are being dishonest at most other times?

The confluent response begins by comparing the choices to candy. Then, the merits and limitations of each choice are methodically exposed. Finally, intelligence is framed as a gateway to all other things. So, it becomes more than itself. Charm is also defined. Then, both characteristics are shown to be vehicles to contributing to humanity. This is a higher value than, say, having a dynamite social life. The concluding sentence returns to the candy metaphor, which simply reinforces the overall effect.

While it's not inconceivable that a young woman might want to have an amazing social life, the judges are looking for someone who displays strong character. So, it is advisable to think about answers in those terms. It is not disingenuous for a contestant to acknowledge that she would love to have this quality or that, but then she should go on to choose something more substantive.

Question of the Day #5

Teachers open the door, but you must enter yourself.

– Chinese proverb

Question. If you were asked to convince an adolescent to read more and watch less TV, what would you say?

Default response. I have no idea, but maybe I would tell her that there is a lot to learn from books.

Reflective response. That's a hard question. I don't really know. I like to read. Maybe I'd show her a copy of Cosmopolitan. That would interest most girls. I guess I would also tell her about some of the books that I've read.

Confluent response. In this day of On Demand TV, Wii, and 24-hour sports channels, convincing a teenager to read more is a real challenge. But, I still find books have something that cannot be found anywhere else. I love holding a book in my hand and the way that ink and paper smells. I love owning books that I can relate to. I would tell her that when I was a junior in high school, I read A Separate Peace by John Knowles. I fell in love with this book. It is the story of two boys at a New Hampshire prep school. One impulsive act has consequences that last for a lifetime. It is a bittersweet story that hangs on the edge of emotion, but never goes over. For me, it was more than a story. The author captured all the confusion and angst of being an adolescent. I saw myself on every page. I read that book six times and still think about it today. As reading is interactive and watching TV is passive, I would tell her to go to the library, find a book—any book about any subject—and fall in love with it.

Coach's commentary. The default response begins by announcing that the contestant has given up. Never begin an answer with a negative. The reflective response has the same problem, but the contestant rescues herself with some decent examples. Telling the judges "I like to read," is a good way to open the answer, but there are no examples. The idea of using Cosmopolitan as a motivator to promote reading is a bright idea, and this could have been connected with other materials that might interest young women in reading.

However, the contrast between the two answers is evident in the narrative quality of the confluent response. The reflective response says, "I would also tell her about some of the books that I've read," but they are not enumerated. The confluent response, however, shares a story about a specific book, and showing is far more effective than telling. There is a succinct synopsis of a novel, which describes its tension and emotional content. In the narrative, we receive some insight into why this book was so important to the reader: "I saw myself on every page." Plus, the confluent response conveys a real passion for the written word and even the physical materials of a book—paper, print, and binding.

The conclusion compares the passive act of TV watching as opposed to the interactive nature of reading. This introduces an important piece of information. It adds an entirely different reason to read. Rather than being restrictive in the ending, the final sentence leaves the choice of reading material up to the adolescent. Everything is tied together with the comment, "fall in love with it." This is a hopeful answer to a challenging question.

Question of the Day #6

Every great dream begins with a dreamer. Always remember, you have within you the strength, the patience, and the passion to reach for the stars to change the world.

– Harriet Tubman, abolitionist,
humanitarian (1820?–1913)

Question. What's the best thing about being you?

Default response. I'm just like everyone else, except I'm not.

Reflective response. I think the best thing about me is my ability to get along with everyone. You can ask anyone who knows me, I get along with everyone. I received the congeniality award at my local pageant. It's important to get along with everyone, because there are different types of people in the world.

Confluent response. I have a few good qualities; one, in particular, comes to mind. I used to run in 5K road races. I habitually finished fourth in my division. Third-place winners got a medal or a small trophy. I usually got a water bottle. By the end of every race, I was spent. I don't think an Olympic athlete put out a greater effort. I would have liked to be the guys who placed. I had the drive but not the engine. However, I never stopped trying, and every once in a while, I got close to placing.

I think life is a marathon, not a sprint. It takes perseverance to be a winner. Explorers, research scientists, and artists have the kind of tenacity that allows them to never become discouraged. Like the inventor, I see every failed experiment as information that brings me closer to the goal. Edison did 10,000 experiments before he invented the light bulb. I once rewrote a single word in a poem 62 times. I hold firm to the belief that the only way to fail is to quit. Yes, my best quality is tenacity.

Coach's commentary. Most interview contestants think that answering the question is enough. Actually, the goal is to tell the judges as much as one can about oneself. An engaging answer is like a good meal. The main course is the narrative. A variety of facts and references are side dishes. Metaphors are a garnish, which add delicate flavor and a dash of color. The seasoning comes from humor, self-disclosure, and humility. The conclusion is a delicious dessert that gives the meal a sweet ending. When done, one is fully satiated, but not overstuffed.

With that in mind, compare the three answers. The default response is the kind of convoluted answer that gives pageants a bad name. The reflective response is more engaging, but it is too brief. With the intensity of a stage drama in the confluent response, the entire answer builds to a conclusion. It is dense with information and personal insights. Then, inventors are tied in to the answer to support the thesis that failure is not failure, only information gathering. Building on this, there is reference to poetry writing, which potentially opens a whole other line of questioning. That demonstrates how seeding an answer with tidbits sets the stage for further questions. The conclusion is succinct and confirms everything that the judges have learned from the narrative.

This confluent response approaches the question obliquely. Instead of going directly at it, a storyline is developed and expanded until it completes a great circle. Read and reread this answer until all of its subtleties are revealed.

Question of the Day #7

An idea is a point of departure and no more. As soon as you elaborate it, it becomes transformed by thought.

– Pablo Picasso, artist (1881–1973)

Question. If you were forced to leave your house but could save one thing (not counting people or pets), what would it be?

Default response. I would take my jewelry box. It has my favorite pieces of jewelry and some pictures of me when I was younger.

Reflective response. That would be a hard choice. I have so many things that mean so much to me. Let's see, I have my computer that has my pictures on it. I have many clothes, but I suppose I could get more clothes. I have my jewelry, which has a lot of sentimental value to me. I also have a collection of Barbie dolls, from when I was younger. I loved those dolls. I guess if I had to choose one thing, it would be the charm bracelet that I have had since I was little. Each charm means something to me.

Confluent response. Actually, my parents lost a lot of their possessions in two different fires. So, although this is a difficult question, it's one that I have actually thought a lot about.

I once wrote a poem called, "Looking for Familiar Names." It's about how I read the obituaries every day. After a while, you learn to read the code: died at home, surrounded by family, and went to the Lord. Each of these has a different nuance of meaning. One day, it occurred to me that the sum total of a person's life—no matter how accomplished or wealthy—comes down to 30 lines in the newspaper. It made me sad, but at the same time, it helped me appreciate what has real value.

I have many things that I love in my house: my mother's furniture, my books, artwork, poems, and so many mementos. I also have a collection of childhood toys, original prints from the author Nick Bantock, my cousin Mary's beautiful flora watercolors, and my favorite book, The Pop-Up Book of Phobias. It would take the wisdom of Solomon to choose between them. As much as I would want to have these, I would take a very old picture album. It contains the oldest pictures of my family. I have a particular

201

favorite of my dad on Thanksgiving, when I made the dinner, and we watched football together. These pictures are like a part of my DNA. If everything else were destroyed, I would mourn my losses and move forward with what I had left.

Coach's commentary. This is a question that requires the contestant to make a difficult choice. Everyone has many treasured objects and mementos. What to choose and what to leave present a dilemma. Most contestants are frozen in indecision by a question like this. Herein lies the key: a contestant must remember that her house is not actually on fire. The answer is not about what she would take as much as why she would take it. Therefore, anything that she considers of value is appropriate. The contestant's task is to convey her thoughts, feelings, and story to the judges.

The default response conveys no sense of emotion or importance. On the other hand, the reflective response is quite well developed and detailed. In the confluent response, the actual object—the photo album—isn't even named until a lot of preparatory information has been shared. This answer is so rich, I could write a book analyzing why it is so engaging. There is enough material contained within this response to keep the judges asking questions about it for the entire interview. Personal stories make the judges curious. What is The Pop-Up Book of Phobias? Who is Nick Bantock? Would you like to hear my poem, which I actually did write?

Further, the choice to preserve the photo album is reinforced by specific references to particular photos. Comparing it to DNA shows how important it is. The final statement displays character and the idea that objects are not the most important things in life.

Question of the Day #8

When you know a thing, to hold that you know it; and when you do not know a thing, to allow that you not know it—this is knowledge.

– Confucius, philosopher
(551 BC–479 BC)

Question. Should schools offer cash incentives to students?

Default response. I think kids should be paid for getting good grades.

Reflective response. I think it's a good idea. Some kids have to work after school. Other kids would try harder if they were getting paid. If you have a job, you get paid. Why shouldn't kids be paid for doing well in school?

Confluent response. One of the UConn Lady Huskies basketball players did a hilarious imitation of the coach during practice. When a player missed an easy shot, she would stand under the basket and shout, "You get a $30,000 scholarship, and you can't even make a layup!"

It costs taxpayers anywhere from $10,000 to $12,000 to send a child to public school each year. This does not even count the students who require special programs. Those are a kind of scholarship, but how many students get the full dollar value? Schools provide sports, extracurricular activities, clubs, and various privileges, and some even give away prizes for good attendance.

I think the idea that education is a privilege and an opportunity to make a better future has been lost for too many kids. They are in school for the wrong reasons. Teachers have to literally beg them to do their work. Paying students for doing what they should be doing is bribery. While it might work with some kids, I don't think it would change anything for the majority. In my opinion, kids already have more than enough incentives to do well in school.

Coach's commentary. The default response, ironically, reinforces the idea that a response is neither right nor wrong. It is in the details, not the opinion, that the interview is won. There is nothing wrong with the reflective response. It presents some valid ideas in support of paying students. It also makes some unverified claims. How do we know if "some kids would try harder?" This answer is devoid of narrative. Everyone goes to school, so everyone has at least one personal story about motivation, which could have added to the answer. Even without verifying data or references, answers depend on a strong conviction and a persuasive argument.

There is no question about the point of view assumed in the confluent response. The answer is unequivocal and compelling. The basketball narrative is amusing and unusual, and it establishes a position before it is explained. Placing a specific dollar value on cost of education gives credence to the answer by demonstrating knowledge of the subject. Direct references to school activities reinforce the point. Interpreting educational funding as a scholarship is not something with which everyone would agree. Regardless, this interpretation is creative and convincing. Acknowledging that financial incentives would work for some students shows openness and flexible thinking. Finally, the conclusion ties the entire answer together into a neat, little package.

Question of the Day #9

Politeness and consideration for others is like investing pennies and getting dollars back.

– Thomas Sowell, economist, social critic,
author (1930–)

Question. What is your weakness?

Default response. Some people say I am a gossip, but I think it is perfectly natural to want to talk about people.

Reflective response. My weakness is that I can be impatient. Like when people aren't listening or doing what they are supposed to do, I will say something. When you are a leader, you are expected to have high standards.

Confluent response. When I was young, the Good Humor ice cream man would come up the street every summer night at 9:00 pm. I would take a quarter from my mother's purse and buy a banana split ice cream bar. Nothing ever tasted as decadent; banana ice cream with chocolate and strawberry swirls covered by a thick layer of dark chocolate. But, as the summer passed, what had been a treat lost its appeal. By the time the season ended, I could barely look at a banana split ice cream bar.

Like this ice cream bar, everything is a double-edged sword. My weakness and my strength are the same thing. I am a self-declared perfectionist, although some of my high school teachers would argue otherwise. I write poetry. After the initial writing, I am pretty sure that the poem is done. I return to do a little bit of revising and to change a word or two. It never fails; I spend weeks looking for just the right words. Once I wrote a single word 62 times before I was satisfied. Is it artistic integrity or obsession? Regardless, I think it serves me well because no matter how difficult, I eventually do get it right.

I admire the spontaneity and energy of many artists. They capture a moment and do not tamper with it. Their work possesses a certain creative energy that is lost during interminable revisions. Well, everyone has a particular style; mine is to revise and rewrite. So, my weakness is that I obsess over my work; my strength is that I will not rest until I am satisfied that I have done my best.

Coach's commentary. This is another common pageant interview question. It is usually answered with some personal revelation. However, a contestant needs to be careful with this answer, as it is not a good idea to showcase negative traits. Saying something that indicates a major flaw in the contestant's character or judgment could put the contestant out of the running. On other hand, an answer that is safe can be perceived as inauthentic. Saying, "I have a weakness for M&Ms" just isn't going to be introspective enough.

In the default response, the contestant reveals some disturbing behavior. On top of that, she goes on to justify it. The reflective response discloses a character trait that is common to everyone. The wording makes it sound as though impatience is not the contestant's weakness, as much as it is a response to other people's bad behavior. It is good that the weakness is qualified by indicating that it is not something that happens all of the time—she made it situational. Still, the response is rather vague, and she implies that she is a leader without actually stating that.

Another way to deal with this question is to use self-deprecating humor. Having a genuine wish to prevail over a personal weakness and some ideas how to do it will soften the impact. Also, as shown in the confluent response, showing that the weakness is really a strength will make it appear far less threatening. Answering this question doesn't call for psychoanalysis. Have fun with it.

Question of the Day #10

One of those days is none of those days.

– Anonymous

Question. What is your guilty pleasure?

Default response. I love pizza.

Reflective response. I have to admit that I love chocolate cake. When I am in training for a pageant, I try not to eat it. But, sometimes I just can't resist. My mother makes the best chocolate cake from scratch. When it's baking, I always stop whatever I am doing and go to the kitchen.

Confluent response. I have a personal Christmas tradition. Every December 24th, I watch Jean Shepherd's iconic film, A Christmas Story. It usually runs for 24 hours on a cable TV station. Like Ralphie in the movie, I had a genuine Red Ryder BB gun. Just remembering it makes me feel good. When I was young, many of my toys came through cereal box offers. For 50 cents plus postage and handling, a kid could send away for tanks, submarines, space goggles, Superman towels, and decoders that glowed in the dark. Nothing was more wonderful than checking the mailbox everyday to see if the new toy had arrived. Those feelings remain with me, which brings me to my guilty pleasure.

I buy toys that I had—or wish I had—when I was young. In 1955, I sent away for a set of three underwater demolition experts. When the set was reissued 50 years later, I had to have it. Although I was too old for G.I. Joe, I acquired both the Navy diver and the Frogman. My latest find is a circa 1960 Tonka bulldozer, which I refurbished. I even got the decals for it in a separate bid on eBay. I also own old time radio programs, like The Jack Benny Program and Our Miss Brooks.

Owning my toys takes me back to a time when there was Santa Claus, six-guns, and heroes, and playing was serious fun. While I don't wish to be a child again, my toys connect me with a world that has disappeared but has not been forgotten.

Coach's commentary. If you don't get it by now, I haven't done my job as a coach. I am confident that you understand what makes a good interview answer. Everybody has a story. All it takes is a sentence or two to kick off a coherent narrative. With practice, it will become natural as breathing.

Think about the three responses to the question. From their answers, which contestant do you know better? The default response lack any flavor. The reflective response contains some elaboration, but it could use more. The confluent response talks about toys, but the subtext is about a person. Among the first things I ask a new pageant contestant is, do you have any hobbies or collections? The story with all its diversions weaves a colorful tapestry of events. An interview answer is like a bicycle wheel; at the center there is a hub. Extending from the center, each spoke adds an additional part of the story, a fact or an anecdote. In end, it always comes back to the center, which is the answer to the question.

Question of the Day: #11

To succeed in life, you need three things: a wishbone,
a backbone, and a funny bone.

– Reba McEntire, singer and
actress (1955–)

Question. What is the best present that you have ever received?

Default response. I got my first two-wheel bicycle for Christmas when I was 6 years old. I remember it because it was red and had a bell.

Reflective response. The best present that I ever got was a Barbie doll. When I was 7 years old, I wanted the Christmas Barbie more than anything in the world. On Christmas morning, I got out of bed really early and went downstairs. We had to wait until after breakfast before we were allowed to open our presents. I looked at all the presents under the tree, but none of them were the right size for the Barbie doll. I was so disappointed, that I started to cry. I ate breakfast with my family, and then we sat down to open our presents. My mother handed me a box. I didn't know what it was until I opened it. There was the Barbie doll, all dressed for Christmas. That was the best present I ever got.

Confluent response. The week before Christmas, a package from my friend's 6-year-old niece arrived via UPS. I had been sending this child Christmas and birthday presents since she was born. Opening the package, the first thing I found was a postcard with her and her younger brother's names carefully printed on it. The card had a picture of a room in a Victorian dollhouse, all decorated for the holidays. The detail was amazing; ornaments on the tree, a lit chandelier, curtains on the window, a staircase, even wood in the fireplace. I still have the card. I started opening presents not knowing what to expect. It was obvious that her grandmother had a hand in this, but it still had the touch of a little girl. There were about a dozen different presents, each individually wrapped: a refrigerator magnet, leather gloves two sizes too big, a pair of dark brown socks, a tiny sled ornament with my name on it, a handcrafted butterfly, a wooden birdhouse, a rooster made of colored glass, and all kinds of candy, some of which I suspect were left over from Halloween. That was fine, since I felt like a kid in a candy shop. I had so much fun opening all the presents. At that moment, I was filled with that sense of magic that children experience and grown-ups try to recapture. Every time I come across one of these presents, I feel like a kid on Christmas Eve.

Coach's commentary. The default response tells about an object, but nothing about the person who received it. The reflective response contains enough detail and description to make this answer engaging. Although the story is a little generic, it is still good. The only issue I have is that by revealing that the present was a Barbie doll in the opening, a lot of the drama is lost.

The confluent response is unique and unexpected. It contains a balance between description and psychological appeal. This answer is filled with details that paint the proverbial word picture. A small degree of anticipation is built with the context of Christmas, the relationship, and the delivery of the actual package. The emphasis is more on the context than the actual items, which demonstrates certain sentimentality and personal values. Observations about the magic of Christmas, childhood, and adult response demonstrate insight and sensitivity.

Was this the very best present I have ever received? It doesn't matter. The contestant does not have time to rummage through a lifetime of memories to uncover the definitive answer. In fact, the very best gift may not make the best story. Interview contestants can take the first random thought that comes to mind and turn it into a captivating narrative. No one will ever know the difference. It is not inconceivable that a contestant could give a different answer to the same question at different time. For example, my favorite song changes almost daily. Remember, the goal is to give an answer that the judges will remember.

Question of the Day: #12

Education is not a preparation for life; education is life itself.

– John Dewey, philosopher, psychologist,
educational reformer (1859–1952)

Question. What's on your to-do list?

Default response. I used up all of my toiletries this week. On the way home, I have to pick up shampoo and hairspray.

Reflective response. I keep a journal, and every night I write down what I want to do the next day. For example, tomorrow, I have to take my dog to the vet and get my computer repaired. In the future, I would love to go shopping in Boston or New York, and I want to enter another pageant. First and foremost, I want to do more with my platform. I love playing sports, and I want to continue going to the gym. I would like to finish my degree in communications and get a job as a TV reporter. I think it's important for people to have goals.

Confluent response. What immediately comes to mind is the 2007 movie, The Bucket List, which starred Jack Nicholson and my favorite actor, Morgan Freeman. If you are not familiar with it the film, it's about two terminally ill men who decide to do all of the things that they have always wanted to do before they die. My to-do list is not quite so dramatic, but there are some small things and some more ambitious projects I would like to tackle in the next year. I would like to join a poetry group and edit some of my poems into a small book called Ice Cream Sundays. Along this literary line, I also have plans to write and illustrate a children's book. While I don't have aspirations toward stardom, I would like to appear in a movie, mainly to observe the process first-hand. This could actually happen, since a movie studio is considering relocating to the town where I live. There are a whole bunch of little things I'd like to see, like the rings of Saturn through a good telescope; go bowling; take swings in a batting cage; and play a round of golf. I also want to learn to dance, like the people on Dancing with the Stars. I recently "roasted" a friend, which I enjoyed so much that I would be willing to give stand-up comedy a try. Coaching a gubernatorial candidate and a Miss America winner are among my career goals. Before I die, I want to endow an educational scholarship. Speaking of education, I want to take a course in poetry and publishing. Oh! There is one more thing—I really want to try one of those Dunkin Donuts pumpkin muffins. I know why they call it a "bucket list." If you did everything in a year, it would kill you. So, there you have it—my to-do list for this year.

Coach's commentary. Since this is the final question in this series, ask yourself, "Which answer holds my attention?" The answer to this question is highly personal and requires a degree of creativity. First, the default response is indicative of a contestant who doesn't get it. The reflective response is predictable. It, too, suffers from being object-oriented. The only provocative information is that the contestant keeps a journal. Conversely, the confluent response demonstrates high expectations and wide-ranging interests. Taken as a whole, this is a narrative that tells the story of a person who is deeply involved in the world. Specific examples animate this response. The judges feel as though they know this person. If there is a criticism, it tends to be a little lengthy. Concluding with the muffin lends a bit of humor and a touch of sweetness.

IV. ASK THE INTERVIEW COACH

There are years that ask questions and years that give answers.

– Zora Neale Hurston, author
(1891–1960)

It is my hope that each reader of this book will feel as if she has a personal interview coach. With that in mind, I have included this chapter to answer questions that I am most often asked. This part of the book intentionally contains short explanations. For a more detailed discussion of any answer, consult the first two chapters of this book.

Question. Are mock interviews a good way to prepare for a pageant interview?

Answer. Mock interviews are an excellent way to practice for interviews; however, to improve, the contestant requires good instruction. Unfortunately, many mock interviews actually reinforce poor performance by providing incorrect feedback or conflicting personal opinions. The contestant should have a solid understanding of what makes a quality interview, methods and techniques of the interview, and one-on-one discussions with her coach.

Question. What is the overall goal of the interview?

Answer. The interview is an opportunity for the contestant to make a personal connection with the judges. There are several goals. First, she should try to convey as much information about herself as she can. This includes demonstrating how she thinks, her values, and her ability to communicate. If a platform is part of the competition, she would be well advised to reference it when possible. The contestant should also be prepared to discuss contemporary issues and current events. Most importantly, the contestant must display her personality in the best light. Don't forget that laughter and smiles are universal languages. The pageant interview is all about making the judges feel good about the contestant. The best way to accomplish all of this is through confluent responses.

Question. Are the judges looking for a particular personality type?

Answer. Not necessarily. The judges want someone who is intelligent, articulate, warm, and friendly. They also want a person who will represent the pageant well. This includes making statements to the press, promoting pageantry, and upholding high moral and ethical standards. People can express these qualities in many disparate ways.

Question. Is it all right to talk about things that I intend to do?

Answer. Unless you are specifically asked about some future expectation, such as "Where do you see yourself in 5 years?", a contestant should limit her answers to things she has accomplished or she is presently doing. The contestant's credibility is easily eroded by talking about what might be, rather than what is.

Question. What's the point of practicing, since I can't prepare for every question that is going to be asked?

Answer. A contestant doesn't practice the interview to prepare an answer to a question. Preparation will help her learn to think critically and to remain poised under pressure. The more she practices, the more intuitive she will become. This means being able to sense the judge's response to her and having the ability to frame answers in a variety of ways. A contestant should try to learn something new every practice session. This is not confined to content. There is both a skill and art to having the kind of interview that will resonate with the judges.

Question. What if I don't know anything about the question?

Answer. If a contestant has absolutely no idea about how to answer a certain question, she may say so. She should just be sure that it is an obscure question, which she couldn't reasonably be expected to know anything about. If she does pass on a question, a contestant should let the judges know that she would be interested in knowing the answer at a later time.

Question. What if a question makes me feel uncomfortable?

Answer. If a question makes a contestant feel uncomfortable, she should explain that to the judges and request the next question. For example, someone who has experienced tragedy or the passing of a loved one may not want to talk about it. Questions about sex, religious practices, or other personal matters may be inappropriate. Feel free to pass on such inquiries.

Question. What if I am asked about something from my social networking profile that I'd rather not discuss?

Answer. What a contestant has posted on a social network is there for the world to see. Hindsight is 20/20. A contestant should think before she does something that she might regret later. If she's asked about something on her profile, though, she should answer.

Question. Should I restate the question in my answer?

Answer. I am not an advocate of repeating a question. After a while, the contestant begins to sound like a parrot. Repeating the question also appears staged. I don't see any reason to do this. If the goal is to have a cordial conversation with the judges, a contestant should take her cue from normal discussion.

Question. Can I ask a judge to restate a question?

Answer. If a contestant doesn't understand what is being asked, it is perfectly acceptable to ask a judge to repeat a question. However, try to avoid doing it more than once. Listen carefully. A contestant can answer a question based on her own interpretation.

Question. What if I don't know how I feel about a question?

Answer. The ability to tolerate ambivalence is an indication of a reflective individual. Most pageant contestants are afraid to admit that they have conflicting thoughts and mixed emotions about an issue. However, it is fine see both sides of an issue. A contestant should show that she is familiar with the pertinent information relative to the question. In such a case, her conclusion would be that she needs more information or time to formulate a definitive opinion.

Question. Is it ever acceptable to give a short answer?

Answer. Yes!

Question. Can I call the judges by their first names?

Answer. Not if a contestant wants to win! This will be interpreted as being disrespectful.

Question. Do I have to call the judges "sir" or "ma'am"?

Answer. That's not necessary.

Question. Can I say, "That's a good question" to a judge?

Answer. Only if it is. Be careful not to appear disingenuous by trying to curry favor to make the judges feel smart.

Question. Should I say what I think the judges want to hear?

Answer. As far as I know, no one can read another person's mind. Since a contestant can't know what the judges want to hear, she should say only what she thinks.

Question. Do I have to begin every answer with a story?

Answer. Not every question lends itself to a personal story, although most do. A contestant should use her judgment, keeping in mind that the judges want to know about her.

Question. What should I do with my hands?

Answer. Hands communicate just as emphatically as a person's voice. A contestant should allow her hands to move freely. If she finds herself fidgeting or doesn't know where to rest her hands, she should let them rest just below her waist, one hand clasped over the other. She may return to this position as many times as she likes.

Question. What should I do if I give a poor answer to a question?

Answer. All of us make mistakes. And, what a contestant thinks is a poor answer may be just right for the judges. Regardless, do not dwell on one answer. It will not make or break the interview.

Question. Should I ask the judges how I did?

Answer. The judges have to make their decision and record their scores. These are private. A contestant should not ask for feedback at the end of an interview.

Question. Can I thank the judges?

Answer. Just as one should thank her hosts after a party, thank the judges for their attention. They are volunteers who give their time for the contestants.

Question. Does it matter whether I am the first, middle, or last contestant to interview?

Answer. There is an old expression that says control what you can and let go of what you can't. Since a contestant's position is not under her control, forget about it. In the end, how she performs will determine the result—this she can control.

Question. What do I need to remember just before the interview?

Answer. Give yourself a break! A contestant should do something to take her mind off of the interview. If she has done her homework and prepared properly, she will look forward to meeting the judges. She should try to be in the moment, listen to the questions, and allow her training and personality to take over. Trust yourself!

Question. My business manager said I should make the judges love me. Is that right?

Answer. Having the judges "love you" is a euphemism. It's not literal, although some business managers seem to interpret it that way. The more authentic goal is to make a connection with the judges. If the contestant is perceived as genuine, thoughtful, and entertaining, she will be liked. Having a positive attitude is important. Leave the love for another relationship.

Question. Should all of my answers be politically correct?

Answer. I am an advocate of always telling the truth. However, candor should be tempered with sensitivity and wisdom. Just because a contestant thinks something does not automatically mean that she has to say it. It is important to recognize that people bring different backgrounds, experiences, and opinions to an issue. Learn to respect differences. If a contestant says something insensitive or insulting, she probably doesn't deserve to win. A contestant can express an opinion or take a stance, as long as she makes it clear that she is not disparaging a particular person or group. Also, being sarcastic, critical, or condescending is not going to get her any points with the judges. No one likes to be around a negative person. As much as anything else, how a contestant expresses her ideas will determine how they are received. A pageant winner is expected to get along with everyone. The rule of thumb is to think before you speak.

Question. Will being in a pageant help me later in life?

Answer. What a contestant gets out of a pageant depends on her attitude. Learning new skills, like interview, enhancing self-confidence, and poise, can be immeasurable assets. She may be interviewed for undergraduate and graduate school and every time she pursues a new job. Also, she can make friends for life in a pageant. As I have mentioned, I think that putting oneself out there takes a great deal of courage. Learning to be a gracious winner and dignified in defeat are benefits of pageantry. In the course of a contestant's life, whether she wins or loses a pageant will not be of great consequence. What matters is how she uses the experience to grow as a person.

Question. What was your greatest moment in pageantry?

Answer. Although I am no longer in the classroom, I am still a teacher. When a woman who has struggled with interview finally gets it, I feel a sense of personal accomplishment. Watching someone I coach win the interview award is also exhilarating. It's not the award that pleases me most; it's knowing that I contributed to someone else's success. When I see the smiling face of the winner, as she waves to her mother, or her father is on his cell phone spreading the news to the family, I feel a deep sense of satisfaction. I enjoy my role as teacher, coach, and cheerleader. I am grateful to still have some of the women whom I coached years and years ago among my closest friends.

As a coach, I am always striving to learn more and be better. An experience I'll never forget occurred when a young woman I had coached was asked to deliver the eulogy at her grandmother's funeral. She called me wondering how to express the deep love and connection she felt for her grandmother. She then shaped a beautiful eulogy, and the way she spoke about her grandmother moved the church officials to say that it was the best eulogy that they had ever heard. For me, it meant something else. I was so proud of the way she responded to a very difficult task. Being able to help so many women on their journey is truly my privilege.

V. CAN YOU REPEAT THE QUESTION?

A Question of Practice

If you want work well done, select a busy man—the
other kind has not the time.

– Elbert Hubbard, author, publisher
(1856–1915)

We began interview preparation about 3 months before the
Miss America pageant. By then, Maria had made innumerable public
appearances. She performed at hospitals, convalescent homes, county fairs,
and sang the national anthem at a music festival. She was a fashion model,
the emcee at local pageants, and the keynote speaker for a convention
of teachers. She was interviewed on television and the radio and rode in
parades. I followed every event through the photo journal that she posted
online. I even specifically discussed her pageant preparations on a radio
program.

Frankly, Maria could have done well in the Miss America interview
without any further preparation. So, why was she anxious to do all of that
additional work on interview? It's quite simple. Maria believed that she
could win. What separates the winner from the runners-up is attention
to detail. Both she and I wanted to take her interview to an even higher
level. With her ability and experience, I wanted her to feel confident that
she could answer any question. I also wanted her to be able to direct the
questions and subliminally influence the judges.

To get her ready, I wrote a series of questions that I knew she
had never heard. These would challenge her in ways that she had not
experienced. They were developmental questions, designed to make her
think in-depth about major issues. There is a halo effect from these kinds
of questions. The introspection and critical thinking that they engender
become a habitual way of approaching all questions.

We used the questions in both mock interviews and her private
sessions. When a contestant moves out of her comfort zone, there will be
a time when that she feels as though she is starting over. Apprehension

and doubt are the handmaids of any new endeavor. Eventually, they will be replaced by confidence and a sense of security that comes from knowing that she is ready for anything. So, we started early enough to allow the growth process ample time to unfold. By the time that Maria left for the Miss America pageant, she was like Secretariat, ready to run in the Kentucky Derby.

Here are some of the questions I used to prepare Maria for Miss America. If a contestant can answer these with a compelling, personal narrative and a dose of humor, she can ace any interview.

- What can be done to improve the ethics of people in government, politics, and even sports?
- If you were a contestant on The Bachelor, where would you go for the perfect date?
- Is it acceptable for a celebrity or pageant titleholder to express a political opinion publically?
- What would you do if a tabloid printed an unflattering article about you?
- Do you think there is bias in the way that the news is reported?
- Can anything be done to make the political process more civil and less contentious?
- How would you describe yourself?
- What's the best thing about being you?
- What is your claim to fame?
- If you wrote a memoir, what would the title be?
- Which is more important: ability or effort?
- How have you shown leadership?
- What is your favorite place in your home state?
- If you had 2 days to show someone your state, where would you take him or her?
- Why should we choose you to be Miss America?
- Do you think plastic surgery gives some women an unfair advantage in pageants?
- How would you describe patriotism?
- What is the best thing you learned in school?
- What is your greatest achievement?
- What can you tell me about yourself that I don't know?

- Should a woman take her husband's last name when she marries?
- What's on your to-do list?
- What's the best gift that you have ever been given?
- Why do bad things happen to good people?
- If you could choose one person to sit next to on a long plane ride, who would it be?
- With tattoos as common as they are now, how do you account for their absence in pageants?
- If you were the attorney for a defendant who had committed a heinous crime and you were able to get all of the charges dismissed on a technicality, would the system have failed?
- Do you support the death penalty?
- A man attended a presidential town meeting carrying an exposed, fully loaded rifle. He had a license for the weapon. What is your opinion of this?
- Would you like to live for 150 years?
- Will there ever be a female president?
- Has the feminist movement helped or hurt women?
- Have men and women reached equity in the workplace?
- If a woman ran Wall Street, do you think the recent financial crisis would have occurred?
- What was your most embarrassing moment?
- Is Miss America an icon or a caricature?
- If you could be great at one sport, what would it be?
- What is your guilty pleasure?
- If you were asked to convince an adolescent to read more and watch less TV, what would you say?
- What has been the best thing about being Miss _____?
- What has surprised you about being Miss _____?
- Would you rather be beautiful and wealthy, intelligent and charming, or athletic and famous?
- Do you think marijuana should be legalized?
- What annoys you?
- If you created a bumper sticker, what would it say?
- If there were an 11th Commandment, what would it be?

- If you had 30 minutes with the President, what would you tell him?
- What do you love about your school/job?
- If money were no object, what would you do with your life?

More Practice Questions

There is an old adage in sports that says that the game is won or lost on the practice field. This is equally true for the pageant interview. Preparation involves a lot more than mock interviews. The serious contestant is constantly gathering information for future reference. This includes facts, figures, and examples of everything from genes to jeans. When I hear an interview, particularly on the radio, I like to ask myself how I would answer those questions.

This section presents a starter list of questions. They are grouped by category. This is, by no means, an all-inclusive list of questions. Anytime a contestant hears, reads, or thinks of a question, she should add it to the list. Not only will these questions expand her repertoire, they will make her think critically.

It is best to practice answering these questions out loud. A contestant may use some of these questions during mock interviews or have someone randomly ask them to her. If she challenges herself, when she stands in front of the judges, she will be ready to answer any question.

GENERAL
- Can you do a 45-second commercial about yourself?
- If you could spend an hour with someone living or dead, who would that be?
- If you were stuck alone on a desert island, what three things would you like to have?
- If you were a character from a book, who would you be?
- If you could excel at one thing, what would it be?
- If you had 48 hours to live, what would you do?
- What is your idea of a great day?
- What country/location would you most like to visit?
- Where do you see yourself in 5 years?
- What makes you smile?
- What do you believe?
- What has been the greatest technological advance of the last 10 years?

- How do you define success?
- What do your favorite possessions say about you?
- If you could start a new specialty TV network, what would the subject be?
- If you won the lottery, what would you do with the money?
- If George Washington played a sport, what would it be?
- What has been the greatest area of improvement in your life?
- What worries you?
- Can you describe a time when you displayed courage?
- What do people misunderstand about you?
- What has disappointed you?
- What gives you hope?
- If you could eradicate one disease, which would it be?
- What is the best thing you have ever done?
- What is your ideal day?
- What is the most difficult challenge you have ever faced?
- Have you ever experienced rejection?
- Who keeps you grounded?
- If you could live during a historical period, when would that be?
- What's on the walls of your room?
- What makes you laugh?
- Who would you like to interview?
- What is the difference between sympathy and empathy?
- Do you think there is life on other planets?
- If you ruled the world, what is the first thing you would do?
- If you were given $1 million, what would you do with it?
- Finish this thought: If I could, I would _____?
- If there were a user's guide to you, what would it say?

PERSONAL INFORMATION

- Why should you be selected as Miss _____?
- What gives you the edge over other contestants?
- Would you be willing to leave school/your job for your year as Miss _____?
- Have you ever read a book that changed your life?
- What have you learned from failure?
- What qualities do you look for in a friend?

- What is your greatest strength?
- What is your greatest weakness?
- Who is your role model?
- What do you do when you need to lift your spirits?
- Can you describe your best teacher?
- What event shaped your life the most?
- Finish this sentence: Life is _____.
- What would your best friend say about you?
- As a keynote speaker, what would you tell your graduating class?
- Are men from Mars and women from Venus?
- What is your preferred way of learning?
- What would you like to know?
- Have you had a defining moment in your life?
- What is your most quirky personality trait?
- Do you have any personal rituals?
- What is one thing you would like us to know about you?
- If someone told you that you look like a Barbie doll, would you think it was a compliment or an insult?
- What do you wish you were really good at doing?
- What was your favorite childhood toy?
- If you could do one thing over, what would it be?
- Has being told that you couldn't do something ever motivated you to do it?
- How do you deal with criticism?
- Have you ever faced an ethical dilemma?
- Are you superstitious?

FUN
- What's on your iPod?
- What is the craziest thing that you have ever done?
- What should every grocery list contain?
- If you could be a musician or singer, who would you be?
- Where would you go for the perfect vacation?
- What is your dream car?
- If you could, with whom would you hang out for a day?

- If you were a cartoon character, who would you be?
- If you could have one super power, what would you choose?
- If you could eat one food every day, what would you eat?
- What is the sound of yellow?
- How does blue feel?
- What is the taste of joy?
- What is the smell of determination?
- What is the most unusual food that you have ever eaten?
- Is there a creative activity that you particularly enjoy?

CURRENT EVENTS
- What is the single greatest challenge facing this country?
- If you were President, what is the first thing you would change?
- Should gay couples be allowed to marry?
- Should doctors be able to prescribe marijuana for medical purposes for their patients?
- Should a doctor be able to prescribe a lethal dose of drugs for a terminally ill patient who wants to die?
- Should the legal driving age be raised?
- What's your opinion of "hardcore" rap music?
- How should the country respond to illegal immigration?
- Do you support affirmative action?
- How can we reconcile the educational achievement gap among the races?
- Should the government provide housing for the homeless?
- Can a student be punished in school for something he or she writes on the Internet?
- If a titleholder is arrested, should she lose her crown?
- Should a contestant be penalized for an inappropriate internet posting prior to the pageant?
- Should high school students be required to participate in community service projects?
- Where do you get your news?
- What do you think of the Electoral College?
- What do you think of identity cards for immigrants?
- What do you think of the economy?

- What do you think of the "No Child Left Behind" program?
- What do you think of increased high school graduation requirements?
- What can be done about underage drinking?
- What do you think of jury polling?

WOMEN'S ISSUES
- How would you respond to someone who says pageants foster stereotypes?
- Why aren't there more minority women in pageants?
- Do pageants exploit women?
- Does the media glorify a false ideal of beauty?
- Is the swimsuit competition outdated?
- Do consider yourself a feminist?
- Should women enter combat?
- Do pretty women have an advantage in the world?
- What is the most difficult thing about being a woman?

METAPHORS
- If you were a sport, what would you be?
- If you were a weather pattern, what would you be?
- If you were a pizza, what kind would you be?
- If you were a stock, what kind would you be?
- If you were piece of jewelry, what would you be?
- If you were a pair of shoes, what style would you be?
- If you were a car, what brand and model would you be?
- If you were a newspaper column, what kind would you be?
- If you were a piece of clothing, what would you be?
- If you were a food, what would you be?
- If you were a color, what would you be?
- If you were a painting, which one would you be?

VALUES CLARIFICATION
- Would you rather be the President of the United States or the first lady?
- Would you rather be a working or stay-at-home mother?

- Have you ever broken a rule?
- Would you prefer to be a poet or a novelist?
- If your friend cheated on a test, would you tell the teacher?
- Would you rather be attractive or intelligent?
- Should all laws be followed all of the time?
- Would you tell a friend if her husband/boyfriend was cheating on her?
- Are you a registered Democrat, Republican, or an Independent voter?
- Have you ever made a difficult ethical decision?
- If you could choose a partner with one outstanding quality, would it be intelligence, good looks, or humor?

FAVORITES
- What is your favorite movie?
- What is your favorite pig-out food?
- What is your favorite TV show?
- What are your favorite pizza toppings?
- What is your favorite color?
- What is your favorite cartoon?
- What is your favorite sport?
- What is your favorite painting?
- What is your favorite time of day?
- What is your favorite book?
- What is your favorite song?
- What is your favorite recording artist?
- What is your favorite fragrance?
- What is your favorite piece of clothing?
- What is your favorite animal?
- What is your favorite photograph?
- Who is/was your favorite teacher?
- What is your favorite poem?
- What is your favorite ice cream flavor?
- What is the best gadget you own?
- What's your favorite board game?

PAGEANT
- What made you want to compete in a pageant?
- Are pageants outdated?
- Who was your favorite Miss America?
- Do pageants create an unattainable standard for most young women?
- Is pageant judging more objective or subjective?

PLATFORM
- Can you tell us about your platform?
- Why did you choose this as your platform?
- What have you done to promote your platform?
- What are your plans for continuing your platform?
- How can other people become involved in your platform?
- How would you respond to someone who said that you adapted your platform just to meet a pageant requirement?
- What has been your best experience related to your platform?

JUDGES' CHOICE
- If you could save one thing from your burning house, what would it be?
- Can you describe one of your most cherished moments?
- What would you change about yourself if you could?
- What is your pet peeve?
- How is your generation different from previous generations?
- How did you get your name?
- What will you do if you win the title?
- What recharges your batteries?
- What's your least favorite household chore?
- What's your dream job?

GREAT QUESTIONS
- If you could ask God one question, what would it be?
- What is your greatest gift?
- What purpose do the arts serve?
- Which of the world's great religions is right?

- Do you think "nature" or "nurture" exerts more control over who we are?
- Do you believe in ghosts?
- If you could be the best in the world at one thing, what would that thing be?
- What is your greatest accomplishment?
- What social issue will have the greatest impact on your generation?

Memo to a Queen

*The limits of my language are the limits of my mind.
All I know is what I have words for.*

*– Ludwig Wittgenstein, philosopher
(1889–1951)*

Before takeoff and landing, a pilot goes through a checklist of things that have to be in place. Similarly, the interview memo is a quick checklist of attitudes and actions that a contestant must have to make her "landing" smooth and seamless. Having it with her will provide a sense of security and focus.

- You are in charge.
- Be in the moment.
- Listen to each question.
- Tell the judges what you want them to know about you.
- Make eye contact.
- Have a conversation.
- A smile makes everyone feel good.
- Let the judges laugh with you.
- Don't take yourself too seriously.
- Put yourself into every answer.
- Tell your story.
- Make it fun.
- Trust yourself.
- It's all about you.
- Go into the interview as if you have already won.

CPSIA information can be obtained at www.ICGtesting.com
Printed in the USA
LVOW04s1416150914

404135LV00012B/289/P